GREATNESS

KIDS

INITIATIVE

CELESTE ELSEY and MELISSA LOWENSTEIN
with HOWARD GLASSER

Activities to Bring the
Nurtured Heart Approach to
Life in Education, Families,
and Youth Groups

GREATNESS KIDS INITIATIVE
Activities to Bring the Nurtured Heart Approach to
Life in Education, Families, and Youth Groups

The Nurtured Heart Approach is a trademark of Nurtured Heart Publications.
For information contact:

Nurtured Heart Publications
4165 West Ironwood Hill Drive
Tucson, Arizona 85745
E-mail: adhddoc@theriver.com

For information about bulk purchasing discounts of this book or other Nurtured
HeartApproach books, CDs or DVDs, and for orders within the book industry,please
contact Brigham Distributing at 435-723-6611.

Cover Art by Alice Rose Glasser.
Book Design by Owen DeLeon.
Owen Visual Communication

Copy Editing by Melissa Lowenstein (Block)

Printed by Prolong Press Limited
ISBN 978-0-578-48277-4

Printed in China
First Edition: 2019

TABLE OF CONTENTS

Chapter Six

Chapter Seven

Chapter Eight

ACKNOWLEDGEMENTS

CELESTE

I want to thank all the NHA trainers who have done the hard and rewarding work of developing, implementing, and researching Greatness Kids Initiatives. Thanks to Mary Martin, who invited me to my first Nurtured Heart Approach training; to Stephanie Rule, who had the initial idea to teach middle school academic peer mentors how to use the Nurtured Heart Approach with their peers; and Karen Calkins, the principal who lent early support to our initial middle school implementation.

Abundant thanks also to Jean Hollowell, Executive Director of the Children's Success Foundation, for ongoing support; to Paula Wick for her editing support during the trials we did to evaluate the GKI; Stacie Lancaster and Shelley Smith, who organized the second GKI trial in Iowa; Yael Walfish, who performed the GKI trial looking at the work's impact in the family setting; Julia Chavez and Catherine Covell-Bellendir, who studied GKI in the special education setting; and BJ Byrd, who implemented GKI in elementary school P.E. classes. Thank you to Shallyn Van den Einde, Marylyn Holbrook, Jill Bernedo, Sue Tran, Cquenaya Zorilla-Reddam, Debra Black, Naomi Blaine, Kaia Hassel, Mindy Blackmore, Micki O'Brien, and Nicole Arnhalt for participating in the first GKI trial, and to Genesee

Salamon, Dana Kasowski, Jodi Guttman, Lisa Ficken, Linette Heimbuch, Vicki Zweibohmer, Shelley Smith, Kristie Morris, and Lori Eastwood for participating in the second trial. Thanks to their hard work and dedication, the GKI is making a radical difference in the lives of children and families and in the quality of social and emotional education being received by hundreds of children all over the nation.

Thank you to my sweet family for ongoing encouragement and inspiration, and for frequent reminders to never give up on our passions: Joe Elsey, Ann Elsey, Michael Elsey, Katie Nuzum, Eros Elsey, Tyler Elsey, Jordan May, Jordan Elsey, Megan Ogas, Mandy Sherwood, Cami Johnson, Iris Ip, and Priscilla Burgi.

Thank you to Howie for trusting me, never giving up on me, and acknowledging my ideas... and, most of all, for the bravery it took to share this approach with all of us in the first place. I am forever grateful.

Thank you to Melissa for her ability to share in my vision and for making me feel confident in putting my ideas into words. Her wisdom and expertise bring this book to life.

Thank you to Alice Glasser for her creativity, vision, and flexibility in the creation of the perfect book cover. Her artistic and relational talents are a true gift.

A special thank you to Brittany Stewart for being my angel.

MELISSA

It is always an enormous pleasure to apply my writing and editing skills to bringing Nurtured Heart education to parents, educators, and others who work with, love, and want the best for children. It's hard to imagine a more worthwhile application of my gifts. Thank you to Celeste and Howie for making this happen.

Celeste, you are a treasure—a paragon of warmth and joy and a dedicated bringer of positivity, support, and enthusiasm. Thank you for trusting me to support you in putting this incredibly helpful and visionary program you birthed onto the page. Howard, thanks as always for your capable management of this project, infused as usual with profound vision, clarity, and resourcefulness.

And finally: big love and thanks to my family (Noah, Sarah, Kai, Will), my friends (aka 'family of choice'), all the kiddos I get to work with and play with (my most important guides), and to my colleagues at AHA!—in particular, Jennifer Freed, PhD, my mentor, teacher, and beloved friend.

HOWARD

I am so appreciative of the zeal and brilliance my great colleague Celeste Elsey brings to all her endeavors. The enthusiasm, life force, and creativity she brought to this project was over the moon. You are an inspiration, Celeste, and I am so grateful that you chose to channel your great intensity into this project. I have envisioned bringing Nurtured Heart directly to children for a long time and you have carved a most important and beautiful path for doing so.

Melissa Lowenstein has been an incredibly grounding force for yet another Nurtured Heart Approach project. Melissa: your knack for facilitating the actualization of a coherent document is a reflection of your vast talent and dedication to this cause. You are always so present to making everything fresh and vital.

Thank you, Alice Glasser, for taking a so-needed lead on the artistic side of this book. You are a master of feeling the heart of a project and conveying that into the cover and the look and feel of the inside pages. I am eternally grateful.

My appreciation to Owen DeLeon for your most talented translations of Alice's artistic leadership into the final print-ready version of this book. You make our shared endeavors unfold so beautifully.

And thank you to our great NHA Certified Trainer community for your amazing contributions to this effort. I am endlessly appreciative of all you do to bring our shared work forward.

DEDICATION

To my precious parents Richard and Erline Burgi: for their tremendous support, and for providing me with a sense of freedom and never-ending love felt throughout my entire life.

— CE

PREFACE

by HOWARD GLASSER

Celeste Elsey has a remarkable effect on children. I first saw this in the form of video clips she created as she was mastering the Nurtured Heart Approach: she spoke to her students with such purpose and power, seeming to stop them in their tracks in the best possible way.

Now that we've been close colleagues for so long, I get it. The amount of heart and love that comes through her words is absolutely remarkable. Her every word conveys both meaning and the great love in her heart that wants so much for children to thrive.

I imagine you've arrived here, with us, to read this book, because you are interested in helping, supporting, and investing in the well-being and success of children. Can your voice convey what Celeste's does? I believe that it can. I believe that deep down, this level of passion and expression sits within all of us. Some may find that this part of their voice has become dampened or muted, and my hope is that this book will help them find and amplify it again.

I've been on that journey myself, over and over—as I've lost touch with heart-full expression and worked to find it again. I have had to repeatedly turn back (reset) to exploring hearing deeply into my heart and listening carefully enough to both see and speak what my heart has to say. I have felt how speaking from my heart rather than my mind infinitely empowers my voice. I've had to work hard to get there and stay there...and I know that when I stay in that game, my voice can hold that very same inspiring power that Celeste's does.

Through Celeste's powerful voice has come the Greatness Kids Initiative: an indirect way of teaching children to love from a place within themselves that is heart-centered, authentic, and real. In our world, where it is easy to fall into a sense of loving ideas, beliefs, and things, truly and deeply loving other human beings can be challenging. Celeste has learned to use the Nurtured Heart Approach to get around barriers to love—and has become a master trainer of people of all ages in the process.

———————————— ✶ ————————————

Schools that have adopted NHA school-wide have negligible rates of bullying not because of zero tolerance policies, but rather because children who are nurtured, reached, and raised up via this approach seem to naturally find that positive alternatives to negative ways of connecting feel better energetically. Of their own accord, they find a stronger level of connectivity with people, a more influential way of interacting, and—as I like to say—a 'better broadband' level of relationship with an ultimately more compelling sense of rightness. Given this new environment, they, of their own volition, find transformational wellness. Transformational wellness finds them.

The Nurtured Heart Approach was born out of my work with every level of difficult child, but the insights that fueled that work sprang directly from my own struggles as just such a child. I was a great kid stuck in a pattern I couldn't get out of on my own; everyone around me suffered, save a sparse few who knew how to handle me. In grade school, I underachieved and annoyed the average teacher—the one who only knew how to connect with me and teach me the vital lessons of life in the midst of my challenging behaviors. Juxtaposed with these habits were a few brief, shining moments where a teacher knew how to light up the runway for my being the best kid in the class. No one could explain it at the time, and I believe had someone been able to share the secrets of the seeming magic those few teachers had, I would have emerged from my fog and been an amazing contributor.

The rest of the Nurtured Heart Approach arose from the wild coincidence of my winding up being a family therapist assigned to challenging children whose families were trying as hard as they could with normal and conventional approaches—and were getting nowhere fast, despite trying harder with every next effort.

Supporting these families sparked a recognition deep in me that was a game-changer. That old runway that remained dark for me in my troubled childhood was lit by my recognition that *the same intensity that was driving challenging behavior* (and driving parents to despair or toward medical remedies to tamp down such behavior) *was the fuel for the child's greatness.* Through working with the energy of interaction, it became clear that this greatness could be accessed reliably through positive means. When this same intensity was turned around with interactions that were both heartfelt and energetically congruent, things turned around in ways no one could have imagined.

No parent or teacher wants to rob a child of their beautiful life force—their intensity. What every parent and every teacher wants is to support children in using that same intensity to fuel greatness and great contributions. Annoyance and frustration for the parents and teachers I initially encountered had sprung from a deep sense that greatness was there, but that it couldn't be reached through traditional methods. Through learning and passionately applying the Nurtured Heart Approach, they had learned to be game-changers with the same kind of power and magic as those few gifted teachers I had as a child...and as Celeste, who every day sets a shining example of how to wield that power and magic reliably and with joy.

Traditional approaches can be effective with 90 percent of children. Almost every one of those approaches is doomed to fail with that 10 percent of children who have more than their fair share of intensity. And anyone who has worked in schools knows well that this 10 percent of students is adequate to turn classrooms and campuses upside down every day of the week. Schools expend massive resources trying to address the needs of this 10 percent, usually winding up spinning their wheels and failing to accomplish that goal—until an approach matches their intensity in a way that transports these same children to being the best in the field. When this happens, that same intensity turns out to be a gift. Fortunately, the same approach devised for the toughest children turns out to bring out the best in the other children as well.

Imagine with me: what if those few teachers who knew how to bring out the best in challenging-child me had also devised ways to bring that knowledge directly to students? That would have been a huge game-changer for us all, supporting us in interacting and contributing from a place of inner wealth.

For whatever reason, the universe chose to delay that happening until it found Celeste to bring it to life. She has worked for years to do so, and this great book—a book for which I've been waiting for a lifetime—is the product of that work. As you bring the Nurtured Heart Approach directly to young people, families, and groups, know that you are making an incredible difference in the world.

— Howard Glasser

INTRODUCTION

by CELESTE ELSEY

I was fortunate to grow up in beautiful settings, with a supportive family. My first home was on ten acres and included our house, my grandparents' house, lots of animals, gardens, orchards, and our family's plant nursery. I had plenty of space to play, roam, enjoy nature and animals, and to use up my large stores of energy.

Later, we moved to a hundred-acre ranch, where I spent time taking care of and loving animals from cats to cows and everything in between; gardening; camping in the hills; riding on tractors; watching sunrises and sunsets; riding horses; racing bikes down steep hillsides; building forts; learning to use tools; staring at the night sky; learning to drive and feeling a sense of freedom. I was a happy kid, had good friends, and loved the sense of humor in our household.

Still, outside of my home environment, my energy and intensity often were misdirected. Some adults couldn't handle me. I remember extensive time-outs and writing "I will not talk in class" thousands of times. I have a vivid memory of a 4-H youth group meeting I attended at the age of nine. The meeting had ended, and it was time for everyone to help clean up the multi-purpose room of a school. I'm pretty sure I was doing anything but helping to clean up. Suddenly, an adult had a tight grasp on my arm just above my elbow and was attempting to steer me in the direction of cleaning up. I remember not fighting the effort but thinking: "Now I will absolutely NOT clean up!"

As soon as the tight squeeze on my arm was released, I darted away as fast as I could. I have no memory of the words that were spoken to me—they probably winged my way in the form of some kind of lecture. Although my arm was not really being hurt, I distinctly remember how violent my internal experience was in response to the energy of the situation.

To this day, my incredibly kind and patient mother reports memories of preparing for me and my siblings to return home from the school day. As her children filed in from the bus stop, things would remain calm…until I entered the room. I've heard her referring to my entry as a hurricane hitting. Although I was not doing anything wrong, she reports that my energy would have a way of engulfing the room.

During my 7th grade year, our family moved to a small ranching community. I went from a large junior high where my class included hundreds of students to a class of about 40—most of whom already knew each other well. The change was hard for me. I recall trying to figure out how I could become more a part of my new school, and of course the easiest and most fun route was to become a class clown. It was a great challenge and fun, and I was good at it. I got so much peer and adult attention for my fearless behaviors that I ramped up my game to include carefully planned, strategic and calculated class-clown stunts. I began to enroll other students in my shenanigans.

The first real consequence I remember for these behaviors was receiving an "F" on my report card in math. The grade was no reflection of my math skills: it was a total reflection of my behavior. Next thing I knew, I was being removed from my 8th grade math class and was instead assigned to do my math work at a desk next to my science teacher during his 7th grade science class time. And instead of escalating into worse behaviors, I chose to follow the rules, do my math, and enjoy myself in my new situation.

As an adult, I have often thought about why I chose to do the right thing in that situation. My answer (long before I learned the Nurtured Heart Approach) was that I felt *seen* by my science teacher. He was kind and supportive of my math efforts and made me feel like a successful student. There was no need to act out for attention. I received attention for my good behaviors.

Although my math grade went up and I continued to behave for my science teacher, my antics continued in other classes and during lunch time. I made jokes and imitated staff members for my peers, sometimes drawing large groups. As embarrassing as this is now, I'll admit that kids would pay me to walk like a chicken in front of the large staff room windows during lunch recess.

Near the end of the school year a meeting was called with me, my mother, and the principal. I had quite the attitude of not caring one bit—at least, on the outside. I figured I was in trouble for something, and that my mother would attend, listen to the complaints, and then would speak to me about my inappropriate actions. I can clearly recall sitting in the meeting waiting for the hammer to be dropped with who knew what kind of punishment. While trying to act "cool" and pretending I didn't care about being in trouble, I heard my principal say, "Since it appears that you have no problem with public speaking, Miss Burgi, you will be giving the 8th grade graduation speech in June." Despite my absolute terror in that moment, I used every ounce of my strength to reply back with a nonchalant "whatever."

My mother helped me write my speech; my father listened to me practice it over and over; and I pulled off the delivery without a hitch. Thinking about this now, I can see that the principal saw a strength in me. Instead of punishing me for using it inappropriately, he rewarded me with an incredible opportunity to use it for good. It made a positive difference for me, and I will always be grateful to that principal.

At the age of 23, I was in junior college taking prerequisites for entry into a nursing program. I earned an A on my first test, much to my own surprise and excitement. Up until that point, I had cruised through high school and college with a B average.

As the semester went on, I not only continued to receive A's on tests, but consistently had the highest grades in the class. Peers wanted to study with me, so I agreed to form a study group. I could not believe that I'd ended up in this role, yet I took on the challenge of owning my success.

Throughout 20 years of schooling, I had never been aware of my intelligence until people around me took notice. And once I realized that I could be very successful in college and get great feedback around my success, I worked much harder and began taking my learning to a whole new level. I had a direct experience of shifting my energy to pursue success.

I suppose I'm fortunate that I figured this out at the age of 23, but this experience has inspired me to seek out ways to show young people their own strengths much earlier in their lives. I don't want other young people to have to wait so long to see their own gifts and actualize them. I want to support children in having inner wealth as early as possible.

Fast forward to my own experience as mother of three intense, active boys. Our three boys were always great sleepers, but when they were awake… oh boy, they had a ton of energy.

Over the years, I did my best to be supportive of them, and to find any way I could for them to utilize their energy and intensity. They played sports, they skateboarded, and they roughhoused non-stop. I loved my sons, I tried to be as positive as possible, and I tried to find the right punishments and consequences for their negative behaviors. These boys were always loving toward me and their dad, they never once said anything horrible directed at us, but at the same time, their energy could be very hard to manage. I tried out popular strategies including Three Strikes and You're Out, charts, reward systems, removing privileges, providing acts of community service, forced apologies, and leaving events abruptly due to misbehavior. Nothing seemed to work for long.

Over the years, I received phone calls from teachers. "You must be aware that your son has ADHD to the hilt," said one teacher; another claimed that my son had started a riot in the classroom and that I'd better get a handle on my children. I received multiple phone calls asking that I come and pick my boys up from sleepovers because of their loud energy. I knew of children who weren't allowed to play with the Elsey boys. After our loving niece babysat the boys for a couple of hours, she jokingly said that her ovaries had shrunk while she'd been wrangling my children.

Fortunately, my boys had many caring adults in their lives—including teachers, neighbors, family members and coaches—who loved and supported them. They've grown into incredible young adults.

When our first son was two years old, I decided to go back to school, aiming at the possibility of becoming a teacher. I attended the local junior college and took one general education class at a time for 13 years. I was fortunate to get a job providing reading intervention and being the attendance secretary at my sons' school. I began substitute teaching and was immediately drawn to working with the most challenging students—those struggling both academically and behaviorally. I began my teaching career as a middle school special education teacher, and my first couple of years of teaching were definitely a challenge—even with all of the support I received.

In 2007, my second year of teaching, my colleague, a veteran school psychologist named Mary Martin, came to me one day with an invitation. A couple of flyers for a talk by Howard Glasser on his Nurtured Heart Approach had come across her desk. She'd thrown the first one away and then, upon reading the second copy more closely, she'd become intrigued.

(I remain grateful to this day that she didn't toss the second flyer!) She, I, and another colleague–Stephanie Rule, a school counselor–all decided to go. After hearing Howard speak, we all knew that this was something that would transform our work and set our students up for success.

We returned to school after that first six-hour training with enthusiasm, high hopes, and a desire to find ways to use the Nurtured Heart Approach in our middle school. Our efforts caught the attention of our principal, Karen Calkins, who quickly got on board with NHA. She resonated deeply with the belief that all kids possess qualities of greatness, and that all students had moments of success where they could be recognized. She agreed to support us in attending our first week-long NHA Advanced Training (now referred to as the Certification Training Intensive, CTI) in January 2009.

We returned to our jobs with even more enthusiasm, commitment, and desire to support our students in being their best. Stephanie, Mary, and I decided to teach a six-week NHA parenting course. We supported each other every single day and when it felt difficult, we reminded each other that we knew this was great for all kids.

We began to realize that *the way we responded to misbehaviors* was the most important determinant of how things would go. Good behavior from our middle school students was more about us than them; our responses to negativity would determine whether students would choose to return to positive behaviors or would escalate negative behaviors. We realized that Howard Glasser wasn't joking when he said that NHA is an out-of-the-ordinary mode of hardball that requires fearlessness on the part of the adult.

Some of our colleagues, family members and friends thought we were up to something very strange. I remember being teased by other teachers: "We know what goes on in Elsey's room. She ignores kids' bad behavior and then tells them how great they are." Truthfully, there were times when I wanted to give up on NHA. Often, it was overwhelmingly tempting to slide back into my old ways. Sometimes I gave in to that temptation, but I always found my way back to NHA. It was clear that there was no better path to making a better world for both myself and the students I was serving.

Stephanie and I taught six-week parenting classes for nine years, and Mary taught with us for many of those years until she retired. As I learned and applied the NHA at home, I saw a tremendous difference in my sons' well-being and in our family relationships. If only I had been equipped with this set of strategies and practices earlier in their lives, their paths (and mine) would have been far easier.

Discovering the Nurtured Heart Approach helped me to reframe what had been regarded as difficult or challenging behavior—in both my own childhood, and in the childhoods of my sons—as a misuse/misdirection of a beautiful intensity that was part of our very being. It was a privilege and a blessing to be able to spare others the same challenges, and to give them access to their own greatness earlier in their lives than I found mine, by bringing the Approach into my work with my students and training other adults to use it.

As Mary, Stephanie, and I worked with the NHA at our school, Stephanie had an idea: to teach Academic Peer Mentors how to use the Approach with peers they supported in Math and English Language Arts interventions. I worked on this for three years, implementing a Greatness Kids Mentor Program that was very successful. In the fourth year, our principal felt it was time to begin using the NHA school-wide (Tier II) for any students needing behavioral support. This led to the development of the Greatness Kids Initiative (GKI), the subject of this book.[1]

The first Tier II Greatness Kids group became known as Greatness Kids Intervention. The idea was to support at-risk students with strategies beyond what was offered to all students in the school. This group started with 14 students and grew to 24 students by mid-year. These students were struggling with school-related anxiety, attendance issues, behavior management issues, and problems with work completion. These were the students that even the best teachers couldn't keep in the classroom every day with an acceptable level of success.

The distinction between the GK Mentors and the new GK Intervention group was that for the first time, I was teaching students how to use the Three Stands of NHA on themselves. Believe me, there were challenges. Between daily successes, students put on vivid demonstrations of just how difficult they could be. I had a couple of fights break out. I recall group discussions where the students just wanted to trash talk their parents and/or teachers; moments when I had no choice but to refer students to our mental health counselor for further support; and negative comments about NHA, each other, and me.

Even as these challenges arose, I held to my own use of the Three Stands in order to manage the group as I shared with these students the ways that they could use NHA on themselves and in all aspects of their own lives. And

---

[1]Multitiered Systems of Support (MTSS) are systems increasingly being implemented in public schools for student safety and support. MTSS includes three tiers: Tier I, which brings core instruction to every student; Tier II, targeted intervention for students who are beginning to struggle; and Tier III, intensive intervention.

in each session, where we met four times per week for thirty minutes per meeting, I saw true miracles happen. Students began to share how they were able to refuse to energize negativity in their own lives. They gained the skills required to see positive qualities in others and themselves, and they learned strategies for resetting themselves.

At their own pace, these students began to choose to behave and participate, and to show empathy and even understanding toward each other. They began to recognize each other positively through activities and then during open discussion times. They were able to genuinely welcome new students into the group who were in the midst of being annoyed and angered that they were invited to join the class. What started out as an idea to support our most challenging students grew into a place where these young people could feel successful. The school principal, our intervention team, and the mental health counselor saw improvement across the board in data collected on all GK Intervention students, including grades, attendance, and behavior referrals.

During that time, I continued to meet with the Greatness Kids Mentors a few times a year. It became obvious to me that these students who, by most standards, did not fit any current description of "at-risk" had basically the same needs and wants as the students faced with big challenges that were interfering with their academic and social-emotional success. These were kids with more privilege: access to extracurricular activities, parents who could afford academic tutoring when needed, exceptional grades, and the latest fashions—and the answers they provided during Greatness Kids activities were basically indistinguishable from those of the less privileged youth. I changed the name to Greatness Kids Initiative to encompass use for kids of all backgrounds, ability, and levels of privilege. At that point, I knew that teaching students how to use NHA on themselves was for ALL kids of ALL ages.

I started to write down all of the activities I'd used with both groups and realized without a doubt that I was onto something important. I shared what was happening with Howard Glasser and other NHA trainers and gave a couple of lunchtime presentations at the week-long CTIs. Interest grew in the NHA world about the work I was doing. When the idea came about to share GKI activities in the form of a book, I was all in—but first, I wanted to run some trials to demonstrate the effectiveness of what I was doing.

The first trial focused on using Greatness Kids activities in school settings across the country. I had a list of about 20 NHA trainers who had shown interest in using the activities; they made up the first trial group.

These educators were mostly teachers, but the group also included some counselors and psychologists. They worked with students of all ages, but primarily elementary grades. Participants were given clear guidelines to follow, including deadlines for completing their teaching and providing feedback for the activities they had been asked to use.

The results of this first trial showed a wide range of success and some struggles. The thing I realized from the first trial is that the teacher's facility in actually USING the approach while sharing its meaning with students (something we will call "being the approach" later in this book) was of the utmost importance.

I investigated use of GKI activities in the family setting and also in a school for emotionally disturbed youth by sharing activities with parents and colleagues and collecting informal data. The response to use in these settings was positive and continues today.

The next trial came out of a training I did in Iowa for a group that included advanced users of the NHA and newcomers to the Approach. Educators, mental health professionals, hospital staff, parents and social workers were included. I had decided to use some of the Greatness Kids activities to share the approach with adults with the intention of increasing their levels of understanding through experiential activities (a major component of the GKI). The training turned out to be one of my favorites ever. The crowd was engaged and asked questions throughout. They challenged NHA and participated fully in the activities. They provided me with honest and clear feedback at the end of the day, and most requested to be involved in the next Greatness Kids Initiative trial.

During both trials, I had just begun a new job, and was leading GKI groups in middle and high school alternative education settings including juvenile hall, as well as leading groups as a Tier II intervention in elementary schools and as a way to model use of NHA for coaching purposes in Pre-K through high school grades. It was an exciting time for implementing GKI groups. I experienced successes and had many learning opportunities that guided me to improved activities.

Greatness Kids Initiative trials allowed me to gather qualitative evidence of the validity and value of the activities. I wanted to be absolutely sure that the activities could make a positive difference for kids with other adults (who weren't me!) participating as group leaders, and that the activities' benefits were repeatable.

An important lesson learned was that to gain the most effectiveness from the activities, the group leader needed to commit to "being" (using) NHA while leading activities.

Qualitative data collected from trial participants included statements like:

* "My students learned how to take a close look at themselves."

* "The participants began to believe that they did possess positive qualities of greatness."

* "My students shared that they felt safe and were willing to share personal experiences in front of their peers."

* "Participants began to recognize their emotions."

* "The youth in my group wanted to give up the negative statements they often heard about themselves."

* "My students began to understand Inner Wealth."

* "My family began to recognize each other."

* "My kids were able to develop coping strategies."

* "The youth began to understand the value of a reset."

* "It was so wonderful to hear kids recognize themselves."

* "The students in my group began to recognize that they weren't alone in their struggles."

My experience continued to be that all kids want to be seen in their greatness, and that some have erected huge walls to protect themselves against the very relationships where they could receive this—especially those with adults.

Implementing these initiatives and supporting other educators, youth mental health providers, and parents in implementing them has become my greatest passion. Through this work, I get to support young people in being deeply seen as successful; in knowing that who they are is okay and so important—in building inner wealth and owning their greatness. I get to give them a highly effective set of strategies for being truly present in the world and being ready to hold the future in their hands. It also equips me to support adults in understanding the NHA as a way to be with children in a non-punitive and meaningful way, even when difficulties arise; as a concrete path toward promoting success and self-actualization in children. It never fails to inspire me to see adults dipping into this radically positive approach, where they get to see the real child, beyond any negative behaviors.

As for me: I'm still intense. I rely on the Nurtured Heart Approach to channel that intensity into creating the life I want and into serving the world in the best possible way. I reset to gratitude every single day, and I am constantly gifted with a tuning-in to ever-expanding levels of inner wealth in my students and my family.

Thank you for being here with me. I am thrilled to be able to share this work with you, and I know that if you dedicate yourself to it, the rewards that come to you will be as great or greater than my own.

— Celeste Elsey
   February 2019

Chapter One

PURPOSE / INTENTION:

INNER WEALTH

When Celeste was a new teacher and not using the Approach yet, she had a student in one of her classes who needed a lot of academic and behavioral support. She gave this kid a lot: she worked hard to support him and his family, even helping them investigate whether he had learning disabilities.

One day she was teaching math and he said something. She didn't hear it, but most everyone else in the class did. Half the students had looks of horror on their faces, and the other half laughed. She went on teaching, as teachers often do in these situations.

Some of the girls in the class had a habit of writing notes to each other; Celeste found a page full of them after class that day. One girl wrote, "Oh my GOD, can you believe what he said about Ms. Elsey?"

Thankfully, Celeste didn't have to hear what exactly he said, but she was *done*. She was *gasping*. She thought, "I'm done with him. I've done so MUCH for him. This is *it*, I've *had* it." She had proof that he was bad, bad, bad. Celeste marched into the principal's office and said, "That's it. I want him out of my class." And they took him out.

It was so clear. He was out. He'd crossed the line.

If you are an educator, this may sound familiar to you. You may have had this experience with a student, or five students, or ten, or 50. It may not seem like much of a story if you are in the same boat Celeste was in that day.

This still happens to her. And she handles it in a completely different way. She gives a reset – the NHA consequence that you will read about in this book. And then she says to the kid, when the offense is no longer happening, "Thanks for not saying inappropriate things anymore." She stays with the truth of each moment. She no longer gives attention to disrespectful comments. She chooses to respond by using the Three Stands of NHA, and she never takes comments personally.

If you're skeptical that this tactic could lead to a better classroom environment in any universe containing actual real human children, hold that while hearing another more recent story that contains the same elements. Celeste was running a GKI group in a high school setting. On day one, she noticed two groups of girls who didn't like each other, and that when one group shared anything, made comments, or answered questions, the girls in the other group made snide comments. Celeste tuned in to try to hear the next such comment, and when she did (from Jessica), Celeste said, "Jessica, I need you to reset."

Jessica replied, "F*** you, Ms. Elsey."

Celeste said calmly, "Jessica, reset," immediately recognized others in the room who hadn't responded, then turned back to Jessica and said, "Jessica, I appreciate that you aren't using bad language right now."

Celeste didn't give Jessica's inappropriate comment her energy. She simply reset her and turned back to appreciate her after she'd stopped the undesired behavior.

Because the group had been working actively with the NHA in the classroom, the girls Celeste had recognized for not responding went to the principal later that day. They shared that they themselves had given Jessica's comment no energy. They were proud. They wanted Celeste to report this to the principal too—how well they'd handled this classroom incident—and she did. "These young ladies have refused to energize negativity," Celeste told the principal.

There were no more incidences of inappropriate language between those girls in that group. What's more, all the kids began to participate more fully. Celeste made a point of saying to Jessica, "I hope you realize you are as beautiful on the inside as on the outside, and you don't have to be a badass to get people's attention."

With tears in her eyes, Jessica said, "Yeah. I get it now."

The two authors of this book who currently work in schools are encountering a level of apathy, anxiety, and disconnection in youth that we have never seen in our combined 40-plus years of working in this field. The systems in place, as they are now, are not working well enough for enough of the students entrusting themselves to it to become educated, job-ready, relationship-ready adults.

Schools are increasingly recognizing the need for social and emotional education in addition to academics. Many programs are being tested, and many are proving to be of benefit, bringing rises in academic achievement scores, less acting out and emotional distress, and better emotional and psychological health.[2]

The Greatness Kids Initiative introduces young people directly to a simple, time-tested social-emotional model that directly empowers them to (as Gandhi famously said) be the change they wish to see in the world. This model, the Nurtured Heart Approach, was developed by family therapist Howard Glasser in the 1990s. Since then, it has been taught to and implemented by tens of thousands of parents, teachers, youth care providers, and mental health professionals. It has been applied with huge success in homes, classrooms, and across entire schools and school districts; and in therapy practices, centers, and other settings dedicated to building mental wellness.

The Nurtured Heart Approach was initially developed to support adults in transforming the behaviors and attitudes of challenging children. It arose from an intuitively 'downloaded' (from the Universe, not the Internet) set of contentions, intentions, stands, and techniques that Howard then applied in his work as a family therapist.

Back in those early years, the methods he was using to support challenging children–often, those who carried a diagnosis of ADHD or other behavioral or conduct disorders–worked so well that interns he trained to work at his Center for the Difficult Child had greater success than professionals who'd been working with families like these (using more standard methods) for years. Persuaded to teach his methods to other therapists, Howard soon realized that writing, lecturing, and teaching about this Approach would be his way to be of greatest service to the world.

The Nurtured Heart Approach has been in active development, application, and refinement for over 20 years. Although it might initially

---

[2] https://casel.org/impact/

seem to work by teaching one party (a parent, a therapist, a teacher) 'tricks' that modify the child's behavior, this does not ultimately speak to the real heart of the approach, nor does it explain its deep and dramatic impact.

What *does* explain this impact–one that has, according to many reports, seemed to 'cure' ADHD? Our hope is that the next chapters will explain this thoroughly. For now, suffice it to say that it is *not* a method of behavior modification, at least not for the child who has all too often become the identified patient or problem.

What it *is: a path to giving a voice of greatness to children who might not otherwise find it* through transforming the way adults caring for, teaching, or treating the child come to view that child and to communicate the beauty we see in them. This revised mode of interaction is designed to cultivate something the NHA calls *inner wealth* in the child.

What is inner wealth? In the most general sense, it's the way you feel about yourself and the language you use to talk about this with others and to communicate internally. Through NHA and the GKI, we want to foster the development of inner wealth that incorporates:

* Internal strength of heart and character

* A deep belief in yourself

* Great self-esteem

* Trusting yourself

* Feeling good about yourself even when life is difficult or when things go wrong

* Being able to make choices with confidence of mind and spirit

* Being able to recover when you make mistakes

The Greatness Kids Initiative is designed, most fundamentally, to make the most crucial aspects of the Nurtured Heart Approach actionable for school-aged children. It is meant to make a child aware of and grow their own inner wealth–and, by association, to see, appreciate, and acknowledge the inner wealth of others.

The positive impact of this approach is directly correlated with the intensity with which the adult learns and applies it–with the adult's level of commitment to 'BEING the approach.' You will learn and experience much more about this in chapters to come.

In BEING the approach with children in their care, an adult utilizing the Nurtured Heart Approach to deliver the Greatness Kids Initiative material naturally immerses children in its positive language and strong, non-punitive boundaries. Children in this environment then naturally begin to adopt it themselves in their own communications with others and with themselves. Greatness Kids Initiative groups are the vehicle Celeste and some dedicated colleagues developed to give a 'container' to this immersion: where adults living out the NHA could support children in developing these skills in their own relating.

Greatness Kids Initiative activities support young people in cultivating positive and resilient attitudes toward themselves and each other. They help kids to care more about school, as it becomes a socially and emotionally congruent space where they know they are valued in a manner that truly lands and where they have an important part to play. They support young people in learning and practicing concretely loving ways to relate to their peers, and parents and to build their belief in themselves. It takes children on a journey of feeling deeply seen and appreciated. It helps them to see the greatness of their character, building their trust in who they really are: someone who is contributing positively to the world they live in.

They learn to cultivate joy and appreciation in the moment and to support others in doing the same. From that space of positive regard for self and others can come a new sense of caring about and bringing more of themselves into their schooling. From that space of releasing apathetic or oppositional thought and behavior, of coming to believe that it is truly possible to be respected and applauded for who they are and for all the right choices they make (including the choices that are simply *not-wrong*), they develop their very own inner voice of greatness.

Children and families today face a lot of uncertainty. They have a tough fight ahead of them. This Approach can equip them well to love and enjoy their lives and be successful in work and in relationships, even when their external circumstances are challenging. It can give them what they need to interrupt the intergenerational transmission of disadvantage and adverse childhood experiences (ACEs). It can introduce protective factors that will last them a lifetime.

We have seen this in real time, time and again: the greater the inner wealth a person possesses, the better they do in virtually every way. The Greatness Kids Initiative will build this resource for the children you serve—and for you.

Before we dive in further, we'd like to clarify some distinctions between the way we will introduce the Approach to YOU, the adult reader who is interested in implementing the GKI with youth, and the GKI curriculum itself. Some of the ways in which it works best to introduce the NHA to youth—ways that make it most useful to them—will differ from the way we will introduce it to you. As we move through the next two chapters, we'll point out some of those distinctions so they don't create confusion as you implement the GKI.

Chapter Two

THE NURTURED HEART APPROACH:

FOUNDATIONAL

NOTIONS AND PRINCIPLES

The Nurtured Heart Approach was initially developed during the 1990s—a time where diagnosis and drugging of ADHD were at an all-time high. A troubling trend was taking hold: a trend that cast the child with behavior challenges as being flawed and unable to manage themselves without the help of medications with a long list of side effects.

The NHA recasts the child who constantly breaks rules and pushes boundaries, and who seems impossible to corral—the kind of kid who is able to upend even the most experienced teacher's classroom singlehandedly—not as *defiant, bad, difficult, oppositional,* or *challenging,* nor the more positive terms like *spirited, sensitive,* or *energetic*—but as intense.

ON INTENSITY —

The more intensity a child possesses, the more power, passion, and (yes) energy they possess as well. Imagine popping a Ferrari engine into an ancient Ford Model-T and expecting the chassis to hold on the freeway without some serious reinforcement. That's what we are expecting when we expect an intense child to just manage themselves without guidance that matches that intensity.

What Howard Glasser found as he worked therapeutically with hundreds of children and families: the child with a normal level of intensity will most often respond well enough to traditional modes of discipline. Those same modes will usually backfire or even make matters worse for a child with extra intensity. This is because traditional discipline usually gives more connected relationship, more feedback, more pushback, more deep interactions, emotion, involvement, and excitement in response to broken rules, boundary-pushing, and disruptions than to rules followed, boundaries adhered to, and cooperative behavior.

The intense child wants and needs *more* of all these things: excitement-laden relationship, pushback, interactions with depth and strongly connected relationship. If they don't get that *more* in response to their everyday positive choices, they'll be drawn to where the action is. They'll act out to get their needs met.

What usually happens at this point is that the caregivers meet the child's escalating bad behaviors with more energy, more richly emotional reactivity, and more drama—expressions of rising frustration resulting in yet stronger attempts to teach lessons, usually in the form of lectures, reprimands, or punishment. Even where the response is not punitive, it will usually give more of 'the gift of us' to the child who is doing the wrong thing.

Think of the room full of preschoolers where two children begin to fight over a toy. The kind, caring, loving teacher makes a beeline for the problem (disregarding all the children she passes along the way who are behaving appropriately); she kneels down, looks the perpetrators in the eyes, touches them gently, and kindly, lovingly explains to them why it's so important that we must share. Even if redirection 'works' to shift an unwanted behavior, it inadvertently gives the child an increased dose of energized relationship.

Where is the teacher's energy going in this interaction? What are the acting-out children learning? (That if they break the rules, the teacher will come right over and be extra sweet and talk to them a lot. And that adults are never too busy for problems.) What are the children who are looking on learning? (That if they want some of that, they'd better get busy breaking some rules themselves.) Children, especially those with intense needs for closeness and higher energy, inadvertently discover that they get so much more through creating problems than through following the rules.

The child is reinforced: *this* is how I get what I need. It becomes a reflex; a pattern; a habit that then has to be consciously counteracted by parents or educators to create a shift.

CHANGING THE PORTFOLIO

Children who are constantly being corrected and scolded end up regarding themselves in a certain way. They come to see themselves as troublemakers. Sure, they're getting what they need in terms of energized relationship, but they don't actually *enjoy* being in trouble, being criticized, put down, yelled at, or lectured. These things make them feel bad about *themselves*. As though they *are* bad.

Something else may occur with our most challenging children. Their behaviors may escalate to points where adults unsure how to manage them will choose to disregard them. They may choose to suspend, send away, expel, ignore, give up on, or dismiss them, end a foster care agreement, or otherwise act in ways that cause the child to feel alone and unseen. The consequences of this can be tragic well beyond the impact on that struggling child: in recent school shootings, the perpetrators created video footage to be seen following their acts of violence. These videos included statements like, "I was invisible to you, and now I will not be invisible," "You never saw me before... and now everyone will know who I am," and "I'm tired of being ignored and punished. You will not ignore me any longer." These children find a way, through the most unspeakable violence, to be seen and recognized.

The stands and strategies of the Nurtured Heart Approach are designed to transform this portfolio that makes up the child's idea of themselves. They do so by creating positive experiences of the self in real-life contexts—experiences where the child feels profoundly seen, primally nourished, and predictably celebrated for who they are and for the many things they are doing *right* or *not doing wrong*.

TOYS R US AND UPSIDE-DOWN ENERGY

Hand a young child a new and complex toy. What's the first thing they do? Only the most unusual child kicks off their new relationship with that toy by reading the instruction manual. No: they start to experiment. What does the toy do when I push this button? Pull this lever? Shake it? Turn it upside down? This is a rapid, enduring, and healthy way to learn: exploration, discovery, experimentation and manipulation. It is natural to all children.

If a feature of the toy is satisfying—in other words, if it gives back a solid energetic response—the child will return to it again and again. If the feedback is less than compelling, the child probably won't go back to that feature. If the feedback is sometimes *extremely* compelling and other times non-existent or boring, the child may go back to it even more often than the one that steadily creates a less compelling response. The element of uncertainty can be especially thrilling. As long as the big show comes some of the time, the feature will continue to hold interest.

The NHA operates on a fundamental assumption: that *you—YOU—*the child's parent or teacher, or any other important adult figure in the child's life—are the child's favorite toy.

Think about it. No other toy can possibly hold as broad a range of interesting responses as a caring adult. Your range of emotions, reactions, moods, and experiences create a virtually endless array of fascinating responses that present themselves in response to the child's behaviors. You can picture them as aspects of a remarkable, complex, compelling toy, and mostly as aspects that respond differently depending on how you are feeling on any given day. Pushing one 'button' on this toy might elicit one response on a sleepy Sunday afternoon and an entirely different response on a rushed Monday morning.

When things are going well, human 'toys' tend toward low-energy responses and minimally energized connection. When problems occur, the responses of these same adult 'toys' tend to get very, very interesting—sometimes explosive. A high-intensity child will intuitively seek out those very, very interesting responses to meet their needs for intense connection. Even a punitive response can read as a reward to the highly intense child who needs and wants MORE, regardless of the consequences. All children, intense or not, read more energy from this favorite toy as greater connection and meaning: as more love. An intense child is not out to get you or ruin your life; they are on a journey of experimentation and discovery, searching out the best possible connectivity with you. Kids equate energy with love; as they notice, again and again, that they receive more adult energy when things are going wrong, they are more likely to position themselves right where that energy is flowing strongly. This isn't convoluted; it's congruent.

If we want a child to follow rules and adhere to what we consider 'good behavior,' and we then give them far more of what they most want—relationship and energized connection—in response to 'bad behavior,' the energetic dynamic is upside-down. It is incongruent with what we actually want from the child. It is like telling the child, "Don't misbehave!"—and then handing them $100 every time they do.

Where a child feels more energized, celebrated, and loved in relation to problems, they learn to feed their need for connection through misbehavior, opposition, sadness, and boundary-pushing.

Reflect upon the last chunk of time you spent with a child or children. Consider what 'buttons' elicited the most interesting and colorful responses. If you are like most adults, you are more rapidly and energetically responsive when things are going wrong.

One high school teacher one of us worked with was struggling to better manage a classroom of challenged learners. This teacher was clearly frazzled and defeated due to two 'kryptonite' kids who seemed to make it their mission to disrupt the group's learning as much as possible. These two kids had taken over her classroom. She'd tried every tool in her toolbox to get them to stop, and their behaviors had only escalated. When asked, "How many kids are in the class?" she responded, "Thirty-eight." When asked how many of these kids were *not* being disruptive on most days, she responded (with some impatience), "Thirty-six." This was not just a very easy math problem: it was an attempt to get the teacher to feel gratitude for how much was *not* going wrong in her classroom. This teacher didn't connect with the massive amounts of success happening despite the kryptonite kids. She was adhering to the norm of giving unlimited energy to problems, and she didn't want to waste any of her precious resources focusing on what didn't need to be fixed.

Children need to feel adults seeing them profoundly when they are following the rules—not just when they are breaking or threatening to break them. This does *not* mean ignoring problem behaviors! The NHA requires complete accountability when lines are crossed, and a consequence given any time a rule is broken. This will be covered later on in this chapter and reinforced throughout this book. For now, the most important takeaway from this section is our general habit of seeing and energizing what *isn't* going well and conceiving of a possibility of flipping that upside-down energy right side up.

VIDEO GAME THEORY

Here's another way to look at the energetic underpinnings of the NHA. Consider the video games that can mesmerize even the most distractible, restless child. A student who can't seem to focus or sit still for two minutes can sit stock-still to play video games for hours. They not only play them, they play them with fervor. While in the game, they are entirely committed to being as successful as possible. They play with all of themselves. Clearly, they have an experience of their own growing sense of greatness in that environment.

Why? Because video games' incentives and rewards are set up to elicit a uniquely compelling level of focus, commitment, and concentration. When a child has any kind of success in the midst of a video game, they receive immediate feedback: scoring of points, sounds, visuals, or other forms of energized recognition. Any time a rule is broken, there is always a consequence, and it is delivered seamlessly, in the moment that the line is even fractionally crossed. The child can always get back in the game quickly to start receiving positive feedback for success once again. Where a player's avatar dies a horrible death in the midst of play, getting back to the positive feedback is a simple matter of starting over. There is no lecture, no scolding, no criticism. The video game is never too tired to miss out on providing a consequence, and it never has a headache and forgets to provide recognition. It's a simple reset. The energetics here are consistently right-side-up.

This leads us to the *Three Stands of the Nurtured Heart Approach*. The Three Stands are the guidelines supported by all the notions described so far in this chapter. They build a powerful container within which inner wealth can be built, and they are the main focus of the GKI.

Chapter Three

STANDS ONE & TWO

These Stands are commitments; they are firm guidelines; they are meant to support you in building the clarity and resolve required for powerful impact. They will guide you as you hit choice points in implementing the NHA and in embodying it as you run your GKI groups.

THE FIRST STAND: ABSOLUTELY NO!
I REFUSE TO ENERGIZE NEGATIVITY.

This Stand entails doing all you can to *not* give yourself to what you *don't* want. It is a refusal to reward or respond to negativity of any kind with energy, connection, or relationship, and a commitment to undoing the child's perception that MORE can be gotten in response to negativity.

Let us reiterate: this is not about ignoring bad behavior! Positivity just cannot take hold without this foundational piece. The child has to be convinced that there is no more energy available in that direction for the rest of the approach to work.

Key to success with this first stand is to learn to *reset yourself* any time you feel drawn to give your energy to negativity. This is a practice of taking a pause whenever you notice that you have energized negativity or are about to. You can then move into a few moments of intensive self-care, usually involving a re-direction of the energy that wants to flow toward the negative into Stand Two recognitions for yourself (more on this below) and others; and a re-commitment to Stand One and Stand Three (more on this below as well).

I filmed a conversation about resets I had with Dylan, a 7th grade participant in my Greatness Kids Intervention group:

"You know that thing I do where I give resets? Do you remember when I first started giving you resets, what that was like for you?" I asked him.

"Yeah, I was like...I would have to get like five before I would stop."

"What would you say when I would give you a reset—don't say the words right now, but do you remember what kinds of things you would say?"

Dylan responded, "Yeah."

"Pretty tough."

"They were pretty hardcore."

"How did you feel when I first introduced the idea of resets?"

"I just thought they were a piece of s***." (He didn't say the word, yet he clearly mouthed the word he had in mind.)

In that moment I could have responded in many ways. I could have stopped the filming. I could have said, "cut" with a lot of frustration. I could have given him a lecture about not using or mouthing inappropriate language in our video. I could have asked him to show more self-control and to be more respectful. I could have said, "We're done. I can't do this with you because you won't behave."

None of those reactions, even though they may have been what I felt in the moment, would have supported me in hearing what he had to say about resets. Those reactions would have given attention to his negativity, and his old belief that this was the best way to get "the gift of me." I didn't want that to be re-energized and reinforced. He could have chosen to make a game out of it and continue to throw in more inappropriate language as we filmed.

So: instead of reacting out of annoyance or frustration, I was able to reset myself immediately. I responded with "uh huh," and then quickly moved on with the interview. I gave no energy to his attempt to fit in some inappropriate language. In this situation it could have been appropriate to give Dylan a reset. I chose not to give a reset because he actually reset himself back to being his best for the video in an instant. We were able to move past his behavior quickly and without a hiccup. He was able to share his brilliance in regard to being reset and even learning how to reset himself.

This was a valuable opportunity for me to give Dylan a recognition showing him that I saw his new and improved behavior and it's not something I would ever take for granted. So, I went on, "Now, when I give you a reset, even if I know it's something you don't want to do, or it's a behavior you're having a good old time with and you don't want to stop, you *do* stop, and you *do* listen and you follow my instructions."

Next, I asked Dylan about his process of responding to my resets. He described it as I remembered it: "At first I would have to get five or six, then it started going down to three…and now, it's just one or none."

I said, "You're right, one reset is all it takes."

"Either that or I just stop."

"You reset yourself. Do you realize you're resetting yourself?"

"Yeah."

I was able to use Dylan's brilliance in learning how to reset himself both to appreciate him for doing so, and to give him 100% of the credit for building that skill with practice.

In this example, you can see how the strategies used in NHA stop negativity from taking on its own life and allow success to unfold without a hitch. I used Stands One and Two within moments of each other to capture genuine comments from a child describing his experiences and to appreciate him for his insights and statements.

— CE

Let us reiterate that the self-reset is a PRACTICE. No one ever gets to the point where they *never* go down the road to negativity! Self-resetting gives you a way back, no matter how far you've gone in that direction. As soon as you catch yourself, you can choose to reset yourself and start again. Don't give the slip-up any energy!

One of the most effective ways to teach students about the value of resetting ourselves is to be transparent in doing it ourselves, in front of them, preferably with some kind of narration.

I was on my way across campus to run a group. Another adult said something very upsetting to me. I was so angry I actually burst into tears…and I had kids to teach. What I wanted was to duck into the bathroom and have a good cry, but I had to reset because I didn't want to leave the kids alone in the classroom. So, in I walked with my tear-streaked face, and I said, "Here's the deal. Someone said something to me while I was on my way over here, something really hurtful. I came here willing to reset in front of you, and that's how I'm resetting." Due to my transparency, the students in our group were able to witness a genuine reset. The fact that I didn't allow my ego or position of authority to stop me from being 100% transparent was a gift for our group.

—CE

People want to see other people in all their realness. Children especially prize being shown this side of their teachers. They see you feeling the fullness of whatever emotion is up for you; they see you take care of yourself; and they see you recover and come back to them with full presence. As you role model this, they can feel more free to follow suit.

I love that Celeste refers to the beauty of transparency. It has been such a gift in my own progression of using NHA for the benefit of myself and others to simply reset openly when something is troubling me – whether it's something everyone is aware of or something I am privately experiencing. Sometimes, I don't even really know *what* the issue is; I just know that some energies are impinging on me, or I'm present to some residue of events of the recent past or anticipated future.

Time and time again I find that if I simply exercise enough presence of mind to say aloud that I am resetting, I can take a few deep breaths, and can most often use that same energy as a gift in the next moments that unfold. Instead of allowing myself to become overwhelmed with fear or nervousness or whatever emotion is coming up—and instead of dissociating from it—I tap into that very energy to grow into the greatness of excitement or some other more motivating, positive emotion. Doing so out loud, transparently, is a gift to myself and others around me.

—HG

YOUR NHA PRACTICE VS. THE GREATNESS KIDS INITIATIVE

For youth in GKI groups, the First Stand is also about refusing to energize negativity. Within the lessons, we'll help them look at how they can make use of this Stand to improve their own lives and relationships: for example, they can choose not to get mad at their parent, or to gossip, tease, or get involved with others' conflicts. They will have the opportunity to make it personal.

For these same youth, the self-reset is part of what they'll learn as the Third Stand. For you, as the educator, parent or small group leader, the Third Stand will be about delivering resets to students in your classroom, in your home or in any group setting. The GKI does not teach children to reset other people, but as the adult in charge, you'll need to learn and practice that skill.

Keep this distinction in mind as you move through these next chapters on learning and using the NHA for yourself, and as you work with the material taught to students through the GKI.

THE SECOND STAND: ABSOLUTELY YES!

I RELENTLESSLY CREATE AND ENERGIZE POSITIVITY AND SUCCESS.
I ENERGIZE AND NURTURE FIRSTHAND EXPERIENCES OF SUCCESS.

Taking this Stand entails delivering clear, powerful appreciations in response to (1) things done right, (2) things NOT done wrong, (3) compliance with sensible adult requests, and (4) any reflection of the child's essence, effort, or qualities of greatness.

When we talk about *firsthand* experiences of success, we mean that they are irrefutably true, in the current moment. We make every effort, through careful wording, to 'insert' the child into the experience of being recognized, appreciated and acknowledged—to capture them being good or being great, *right now.* We want to say things deeply and meaningfully enough that the child feels profoundly seen and valued.

By contrast: if we were to say, "Wouldn't it be nice if you were being thoughtful?" or "Can you be respectful?" energetically implies that the child is *not* being these qualities in the current moment. The child perceives this as receiving the gift of relationship through negativity. The Stand Two techniques we will be teaching you shortly will give congruent relationship through a clear expression of your true gratitude *during moments where these qualities— respect, thoughtfulness—are being embodied and lived out by the child.*

The Second Stand is upheld by specific intentions and techniques. Let's look at the intentions first.

BABY STEPS: CREATING SUCCESSES THAT WOULD NOT OTHERWISE EXIST

Picture a baby taking its first toddling steps. They hold on, let go, take a step, then another, then: Plop! Down they go. What do you say? "Your form was lacking there, kiddo. You could have taken at least a few more steps on that try!" Of course not. You're thrilled! "You DID it!" you might cry. You might laugh with delight and burst out with encouraging words as they pull themselves up to try again. Your heart sings; you are totally connected to the efforts of this precious little person. You celebrate every new try and every step forward as the baby continues to practice this new thing called walking. You radiate appreciation and enthusiasm.

It's likely that you've been encouraging even the lead-ups to taking those first few steps: pulling up, balancing, kicking, wiggling—knowing that all of it is in preparation for the confident strides to come. Even with babies who are developmentally different, who might never walk normally, adults are drawn instinctively to take this optimistic, enthusiastic stance of encouragement.

This is the spirit in which we ask you to view the efforts of every child to do all the things a child is called upon to do every day just to develop, learn, and grow.

As babies grow into toddlers and children, adults tend to lose touch with this profoundly grateful, connected state. We begin to grow more in our expectations; to take more for granted; and, possibly, we may become more and more critical. We begin to lecture, cajole, and give pep talks about how the child could be doing better.

As you begin to work with Stand Two, hold the children in your care in the same attitude of wonder that came through when they were babies taking their first steps. Feel in your heart and in your body that same sense that the baby can do no wrong: no strict expectations, just joy and awe in the moment; no bar held high, just an attentive, heart-open state where every movement toward striding free is worthy of recognition, appreciation, acknowledgement and celebration.

Every one of us still contains that innocent, pure baby self. See it in the children you parent, counsel or teach. See their greatness shining through; see their beautiful drive to evolve and grow. Especially in moments where it feels incredibly hard to bring that spirit of acknowledgement to the fore, continue to feel into that notion that successes are always right there to acknowledge. As we allow ourselves to see the beauty of that first inkling of movement in the desired direction, we become a vital part of creating successes that might not otherwise exist. The entire tree exists within the acorn; the entire plant exists within the seed; and vast greatness exists within every child.

During the very first GK Intervention group, we had Ben, an 8th grader new to our school, join us. His cumulative file was very thick; he'd struggled with behavior issues and lack of success throughout his years in school. Ben began every session with his arms crossed on the table and his head down between his arms. As we moved through activities, Ben would always say "pass" with his head down on the table, and I'd recognize him for following my rules and participating. [3]

About two weeks into our eight-week session, students were taking turns sharing things they were grateful for that they had never even really thought about. They were sharing things like: having a mother, being healthy, being safe, being able to sleep in their own bed, having brothers and sisters, living with both parents, getting to go to school, getting to breathe fresh air during PE, being away from temptation, having clothing, and having a home. When it came to Ben's turn, he lifted his head and said, "I'm glad to be alive."

Everyone in the room snapped to attention, caught off guard. It was a pivotal moment—not only in our activity, but for Ben. In the moment, he didn't seem resistant to recognitions, so I unleashed a torrent of positive recognitions on him in front of his peers. I recognized him for sitting up, for choosing to participate fully, and for making a comment so filled with wisdom.

He held his head high and appeared to own his wisdom—and from then on, he always participated fully. Never once after that did he put his head down during group sessions.

—CE

THE TOLL TAKER : CHOOSING HOW WE SEE THINGS

One morning, a man drives across the San Francisco Bay Bridge. He comes to the line of toll booths and notices a toll taker who is behaving differently from the others—dancing energetically in his small cubicle. Curious, the man pulls into the toll taker's lane, and up to the window. Upbeat music plays from a boombox inside the booth.

"Good morning!" the man says. "You look like you're having a great time in there."

"Yes!" the toll taker says. "I have the best job in the world. I have this incredible view. I just got to see the sun rise, and other days, I get to watch it set. Besides that, I'm listening to my favorite tunes and I'm studying to be a professional dancer...and I get paid to practice!"

The man cranes his neck to peer at other toll takers lined up along the bridge's many lanes. "The others don't look nearly as happy as you do."

---

[3] It's important to note that at that time, in 2013, I was still working on my ability to reset myself 100 percent when feeling frustrated with students. Most of the time I was able to show no frustration or annoyance, but underneath my ability to reset myself and give recognitions to Ben for simply saying "pass" even though his head was on the table caused me a good bit of frustration. I can be a control freak when I'm leading a group or teaching a class. I prefer students to be sitting up, facing me and participating fully. And if I had not been able to genuinely recognize Ben for being in group each day and saying "pass," I could have blown my chance to build a positive relationship with him. My patience and willingness to recognize him for even the smallest success was a gift for him. That was what he needed to begin to grow his Inner Wealth. Ben went on to make friends in school, to become more engaged in his school work, and to demonstrate improved behavior and grades.

"Oh, those guys in the stand-up coffins?" the toll taker snaps back. "They're no fun."

Your world, your reality, your interpretation, your choice: you can choose to be the guy in the stand-up coffin, dreading days filled with traffic, noise, drudgery, and exhaust fumes; or you can be the dancing toll taker, creating a space of joy for yourself to inhabit—wherever you happen to be.

We get to choose how we see things, just like the dancing toll taker. We can choose, moment to moment, to see unfolding beauty. Contrary to what some might seem to believe, we are not held captive by other ways of seeing the world.

This goes beyond conventional ideas about cups half-empty or half-full. Even if a cup is *completely* empty, we can choose to imagine what has been in it, or what could be. We are only limited by the power of our imaginations and our willingness to choose, over and over, to see the world through a lens of optimism and gratitude. It begins with our ability to recognize even the smallest things going well around us, in any given moment; and to make a point of appreciating them both out loud and internally.

MIRACLES FROM MOLECULES: PIXELATING SUCCESS

The ability to detect, magnify, and tackle problems is an important part of our genetic birthright. An ability to make mountains from molehills translates to an ability to detect prospective threats to the immediate and long-term safety of ourselves and those we care about. But this human talent can backfire when it comes to relating to children in the ways that best foster their development.

Let's say you notice a child just beginning to cause a disruption in the classroom. Where does your mind go? Perhaps it becomes very busy constructing worst-case scenarios about everything that could go wrong, but the truth is that so far, no actual line has been crossed.

Our culture sanctions catastrophic thinking 100 percent, and it's considered especially wise to think this way if the child in question is a frequent rule-breaker. It's natural that you would start to try to generate an action plan in case things escalate. Unfortunately, this usually leads to an attitude on your part that you may not think the child can read, but that they almost certainly can.

In one famous study, teachers were told, at the start of the year, that certain kids were incredibly gifted (based on a test the researchers administered) and that they shouldn't treat those kids any differently. At year's end, these 'gifted' students outperformed their classmates in virtually every way. The punchline: those students had been chosen randomly. They were no more or less gifted than anyone else in the room.

The take-home here is that your students most definitely can feel whether you're *making mountains from molehills* (focusing and expanding upon mistakes, missteps, and misbehaviors) or *miracles from molecules* (focusing and expanding upon greatness, goodness, what's going well, and every increment toward good choices). This works the same way in a family or in any youth group setting. Our expectations of children matter, and if we choose to expect greatness, we will find it, and the children we teach will know that this is what is in our hearts when they are in our classroom.

Miracles from molecules is about re-directing our prodigious talents for seeing what's wrong toward finding success, goodness, and greatness in this very moment. It's about actively searching out and using language that expresses gratitude where problems are *not* happening; about growing our skills at celebrating children's choices when they are *not* breaking rules, arguing, fighting, acting out, or refusing requests?

Remember that teacher's classroom where 36 of 38 students were *not* 'kryptonite' to the teacher's efforts to educate them: and this meant that there was a great abundance of the miraculous to find, break down into its smallest components, and celebrate in detail.

The NHA has another couple of ways to describe this: breaking it down and adding it up, and pixelation:

* *Break it down, add it up:* This means breaking down even small, insignificant, everyday behaviors into the smallest possible parts to find positives to energize. Where a kid walks into the classroom with his backpack, goes to his seat, and sits down, a lot more has happened and is happening than we usually acknowledge. He had to get up on time; he had to get himself dressed; he had to put everything into his backpack that he needed for school; he had to catch the bus or leave home on his bike or on foot to get to class before the bell. All of these are accomplishments that can be acknowledged, and—if they had *not* happened—they would have yielded a much bigger set of challenges for that child, and maybe for you as well.
* *Pixelation:* "Pixel" is short for "picture element," the smallest unit of

a digital image. The more we zero in on individual pixels, the more becomes visible in that image. With the amazing focusing power of even regular iPhone cameras, zooming in to see more detail is more compelling than it's ever been.

Adopt a practice of breaking it down to add it up; of making miracles from molecules instead of mountains from molehills; think of pixelating what you see to get more clear about things you can energize that either *aren't going wrong* or *are going right.* In the next section, you will learn how to add to this pixelation detailed acknowledgements of character traits — qualities of greatness— that are reflected and revealed by the child's every positive choice.

By 'positive choice,' we mean the vast realm of *every single choice made to follow rules and to not engage in negative behaviors.* As you begin to look for the positive, you'll find that even those 'kryptonite kids,' the worst troublemakers in your classroom or in your home, spend the majority of their time making positive or neutral choices. The word *choice* is a vital ingredient here. Recognize that every single moment of positive or neutral behavior is *chosen* by the child and that this can be acknowledged with gratitude.

After all: if this same child were choosing to do any number of 'wrong things,' we most likely wouldn't hesitate to give them full credit. We can choose instead to give credit to all the hidden pixels of success.

TIME-IN AND TECHNIQUES FOR UPHOLDING THE SECOND STAND

Standard instructions for time-out usually involve the child being removed from the situation and remanded to a time-out spot for a predetermined period of time. Sometimes time-outs work to stop an unwanted behavior; sometimes they don't; and sometimes they lead to an escalating battle as the child refuses to go to the spot or stay there.

The main element missing from most modes of time-out is something the NHA calls "time in." Time-in describes the vital, vibrant space of being successful and being seen and acknowledged in that success. It's the players in the thick of the athletic competition, focused and doing their best and feeling the thrill of contribution. It's the child who is applying themselves with diligence to the schoolwork or chore at hand.

Anyone who is experiencing positive feedback for their presence or their participation is in time-in.

Without time-in, it's hard to care too much about being put in time-out—especially if you're an intense kid who enjoys the excitement of rule-breaking, and to whom no similarly exciting alternative (like time-in) has been made available.

These techniques, when used in the spirit of the intentions and concepts already laid out, will cultivate a delightful and exciting time-in for young people in your classroom, home or GKI groups. They are actionable tools to guide you in building your own way of 'being' the Approach.

Let's say you've already established yourself firmly within the First Stand: you are *not* giving energy and a relationship to negativity, as you may have in the past; and you are ready to begin consistently and actively appreciating and supporting its converse (positive or neutral behavior) by using these techniques.

It's best to start with the first appreciation technique in the list and practice it for a while before building into the second, third, and fourth. Keep in mind at all times that the *timing* of any of these recognitions comprises a huge part of their impact. Simply making a point of dipping into connection mode with a child who is being successful in some everyday way, rather than waiting until something's about to go awry, will start to flip upside-down energy. These techniques are designed to give you ample opportunities to take advantage of the truth of the moment—to empower you to play out Stand Two, even with the most difficult and resistant children.

Another important point about timing: the only time that "time-in" is not available to a young person is when they are actively breaking a rule. Where that is happening, the NHA-appropriate response is a brief, un-energized reset—something that will be thoroughly explained in Chapter Three.

THE THIRD STAND RESET: AN INTRODUCTION

Know that getting Stands One and Two activated will go a long way toward reducing the behaviors you don't want to see in your classroom, family, or youth group. Ground into your stand to *not* give negativity any bandwidth. If a child does break a rule, simply say, as unceremoniously as possible, to the child who is rule-breaking: "[Child's name], reset," and briefly withdraw your energy and connection. Devote some corner of your attention to the child and as soon as you notice them no longer breaking the rule, come back with a recognition of that new reality. "[Child's name], I see you're no longer kicking the leg of your neighbor's chair. Great job resetting—you're now showing respect for their space."

A reminder: Kids participating in the GKI will not learn to reset others, although they will get used to being reset by you and other teacher/leaders. For them, the Third Stand will be about resetting themselves. Second Stand recognitions will be taught to them in a greatly simplified form as well—one appropriate for them to use on themselves, but not designed to shape others' behaviors in quite the way these techniques do.

Knowing that we will develop the Third Stand further later on, let's look at the Second Stand techniques—all geared to accelerate the great positive influence of appreciation and recognition and to best create that rich time-in—in detail.

Active Recognition: Watch carefully for anything positive or neutral to recognize. Then, describe to the child you are recognizing what you see, using as much clarity and detail as possible. Use lead-ins like "I see…" "I hear…" "I notice…" "Here's what I'm sensing…" "Sounds like…" or "Seems to me like…"

* Jordan, I see you working well with your friend and sharing the materials for the project.
* Tyler, I hear you speaking clearly and with plenty of volume when you are called on.
* Michael, I notice you seem frustrated by the assignment and are staying focused. I see you managing your emotions—that's not easy to do.

Avoid speaking specifically to value judgments; stay with the absolutely incontrovertible facts. Active Recognition is particularly powerful for acknowledging children's emotional states and any self-control they may be showing in not acting out challenging emotions. This is a great way to bolster emotional intelligence.

* Sarah, I saw you were sad when your friend said something hurtful. I saw your self-control and that you handled your strong emotions.
* Noah, you had every right to be angry just then. You handled that wave of feeling in a flash. I saw you seriously reaching deep to reset.

Don't be surprised if kids react badly to these recognitions at first. In particular, children who are used to only being seen or energized when misbehaving may push back or escalate in response. If you've been disciplined about refusing to give negativity any energy, this testing may be even more likely. Trust that resistance like this is a sign that what you are doing is beginning to work. No one likes to have their system for getting what they need disrupted; they are likely to feel insecure until they figure out that there's a new way to meet their needs for connection.

We start with Active Recognition because it's the least confronting of all the techniques. If the facts spoken are incontrovertible, you can calmly relate in response to any argument: "I know it's weird for me to say so much about what you are doing well. I noticed I'd been putting a lot of energy and attention on what you *weren't* doing well…and I realized that you do SO much more right than you do wrong. So I'm working on talking about those things instead. I'm sorry it's uncomfortable for you—it is for me, too, a little!—and I hope that shifts for you soon." Don't back down; if you can, ramp up your recognitions to whatever level is required to meet the intensity of the child.

I was new to using NHA and was practicing using Active Recognition in a 7th grade math intervention class I taught. I told my aide what I was doing; although she wasn't quite sure about what I was attempting to do, she remained supportive.

I began class the same way every day. The routine included each student entering, picking up a pencil and their math notebook, taking a seat, and solving the daily practice problems on the board. As students entered, followed the routine, and began solving the daily practice, I moved about the room simply stating what I was seeing in the moment. I said things like, "Oh, I see you're already on number two, thank you" and "Wow, you have your pencil and notebook ready to go," and "Thanks for being in your seat." I was trying very hard to get used to saying what I was seeing in the moment. Although it was hard for me to say exactly what I was seeing instead of "good job," "well done," and "thank you," I had vowed to give every single student an Active Recognition in each class period, and I was going to do my best to keep my word to myself.

I came to a student that appeared to have NOTHING right going on in the moment. Today, as an experienced user of NHA, I can look back and say there was so much going well. Even though his notebook and pencil were still on the back counter, and he was leaning over his chair to loudly tell the story of what had happened at the park the night before, I can see now that I could have recognized him for being in class and being in his seat. That day, instead, as I moved toward him searching inside my head for a proper Active Recognition and feeling a sense of hopelessness, I said, "Oh, I see you have warm shoes on today. It's cold outside."

I saw my aide looking at me and rolling her eyes, but I realized immediately that my "funny" recognition had stopped this student in his tracks. He looked at me like, "what did you just say?" and in that moment I saw that he knew I really saw him. I had proven it by speaking the truth of the moment.

My aide (who is a very close friend) and I still laugh about this attempt at Active Recognition. On that day, I learned that what we say about the positive truth of the moment isn't really what matters. What does matter is the ability to be present enough to see what's going well and then to say it out loud.

— CE

Experiential Recognition: This technique entails adding to Active Recognitions an additional comment about what the child's behavior reveals about who they are. The NHA refers to those qualities as *qualities of greatness,* and they are native to the child—an integral part of their being. You can also see these qualities as *values* the child is upholding through the behavior. By acknowledging lived values with enthusiasm in the moment they *are* being upheld, we support the child's expression of those values far more effectively than we would with any admonishment given when they are not being expressed.

To give an Experiential Recognition, we describe specifically what the child is *doing,* and then we describe what specific *qualities of greatness* within the child are reflected in that action or behavior. A starter list of such qualities can be found on pages 53-54 of this book.

As I began using Experiential Recognition, I felt at times as though I was not being genuine at all. I had been told to make the recognitions my own, yet I struggled *building my greatness vocabulary* enough to be able to come up with recognitions on the fly. For a while, almost every time I gave an Experiential Recognition, it was for "self-control." This worked — because just about any good behavior in my classroom could qualify as demonstrating great self-control.

I want adults to know that it's okay to start small and to lean on just a few easy-to-access Experiential Recognitions. As you develop your skills with practice, your greatness vocabulary will expand. You'll become expert at seeing what's going well, and at accessing a wide range of positive qualities to use for these recognitions.

— CE

QUALITIES OF GREATNESS: A NON-COMPREHENSIVE LIST

Use this list as a starting point for Experiential Recognitions. No such list could capture every expression possible through the heart, so allow your own versions to freely flow. Compliments of this nature will flow with authenticity when you let your heart have a voice.

You might post this list in a prominent place to aid your natural adeptness in deriving experiential recognitions. Every time you pass by it, you might choose a quality to energize with children in your care that day. Consult it when you aren't sure what word to use to reflect their greatness in the moment.

Most of all: consult your heart. You'll be amazed at how you can almost always find a way to see most any one of those qualities being expressed by children in your care.

Acceptance	Adaptability	Altruism	Attractiveness
Abundance	Adoration	Appreciation	Audacity
Accomplishment	Adventure	Approachability	Availability
Accountability	Affection	Artistry	Awareness
Accuracy	Agility	Assertiveness	Balance
Achievement	Alertness	Attentiveness	Beauty

Bliss
Boldness
Bravery
Buoyancy
Calmness
Candor
Capability
Care
Celebrity
Certainty
Charity
Charm
Cheerfulness
Clarity
Cleanliness
Cleverness
Closeness
Comfort
Commitment
Community
Compassion
Competence
Completion
Composure
Concentration
Confidence
Conformity
Congruency
Connection
Consciousness
Conservation
Consistency
Contentment
Continuity
Contribution
Control
Conviction
Cooperation

Courage
Courtesy
Craftiness
Creativity
Credibility
Cunning
Curiosity
Daring
Decisiveness
Delight
Dependability
Depth
Determination
Devotion
Dexterity
Dignity
Diligence
Direction
Directness
Discipline
Discovery
Discretion
Diversity
Dominance
Drive
Duty
Dynamism
Eagerness
Ease
Economy
Efficiency
Elegance
Eloquence
Empathy
Encouragement
Endurance
Energy
Enjoyment

Entertainment
Enthusiasm
Excellence
Excitement
Exhilaration
Expertise
Exploration
Expressiveness
Exuberance
Fairness
Faith
Family
Fascination
Fearlessness
Ferocity
Fidelity
Independence
Flexibility
Flow
Focus
Frankness
Freedom
Friendliness
Friendship
Frugality
Fun
Generosity
Giving
Grace
Gratitude
Growth
Guidance
Happiness
Harmony
Health
Heart
Helpfulness
Heroism

Honesty
Honor
Hopefulness
Hospitality
Humility
Humor
Imagination
Impact
Individuality
Ingenuity
Inquisitiveness
Insightfulness
Inspiration
Integrity
Intelligence
Intensity
Intimacy
Introspection
Intuition
Intuitiveness
Inventiveness
Joy
Judiciousness
Justice
Keenness
Kindness
Knowledge
Leadership
Learning
Lightness
Liveliness
Logic
Longevity
Love
Loyalty
Mastery
Maturity
Meaning

Mellowness	Reasonableness	Spontaneity
Meticulousness	Recognition	Spunk
Mindfulness	Recreation	Stability
Modesty	Refinement	Status
Motivation	Reflection	Stealth
Neatness	Relaxation	Stillness
Nonconformity	Reliability	Strength
Obedience	Relief	Structure
Open-Mindedness	Resilience	Success
Optimism	Resolution	Support
Order	Resolve	Surprise
Organization	Resourcefulness	Sympathy
Originality	Respect	Teamwork
Outrageousness	Responsibility	Thankfulness
Patience	Restraint	Thoroughness
Passion	Reverence	Thoughtfulness
Peace	Richness	Thrift
Perceptiveness	Rigor	Tranquility
Perfection	Satisfaction	Transcendence
Perseverance	Security	Trust
Persistence	Self-Care	Trustworthiness
Persuasiveness	Self-Control	Understanding
Playfulness	Selflessness	Unflappability
Pleasantness	Self-Reliance	Uniqueness
Potency	Self-Respect	Unity
Power	Sensitivity	Valor
Practicality	Serenity	Vigor
Pragmatism	Service	Vision
Precision	Sharing	Vitality
Preparedness	Shrewdness	Vivacity
Presence	Silliness	Warmth
Pride	Simplicity	Watchfulness
Privacy	Sincerity	Wisdom
Proactivity	Skillfulness	Wittiness
Punctuality	Solidarity	Wonder
Rationality	Solitude	Zeal
Realism	Speed	
Reason	Spirituality	

For example (qualities of greatness/values bolded):

* Alice, I see you working well with your friend and sharing the materials for the project. This shows me your great qualities of **fairness** and **generosity.**
* Tristan, I hear you speaking clearly and with plenty of volume when you are called on—I see the greatness of your **courage** to speak up and make sure your words are heard...and your **sincerity** as you share what you really think about the topic we are discussing. Great **authenticity** and **articulateness.**
* Kai, I notice you seem frustrated by your homework and are staying focused. I see you managing your emotions—that's not easy to do. I see you living out your **restraint, perseverance,** and **unflappability** here, and that's helping your brothers stay more focused too.

Experiential Recognitions are a fantastic way to introduce new descriptive language to children—either through acknowledging the moments in which the child is handling their wide variety of emotional states (is the child frustrated? Flustered? Anxious? Disappointed? Dissatisfied? Disgruntled?) or through learning new words describing qualities of greatness or values. Being described to myself while I'm in the midst of purely, non-harmfully expressing an emotion or quality of greatness downloads that new language in a way no worksheet or vocabulary lesson ever could.

Proactive Recognition: Traditional discipline involves talking about rules mostly when they are broken or under threat of being broken. In the NHA, the main reason for rules is to provide vast potential for positive recognitions. *Any* time *any* rule is not being broken, we can give positive acknowledgements about the greatness that choice represents. To give a Proactive Recognition, give appreciation specifically for a rule not being broken, plus an experiential recognition:

* For a very young child: Julian, you are making a great choice right now to not throw the blocks. You're being cooperative and playing in a way that helps all the kids feel safe in the toy area.
* For an elementary schooler: Jennifer, I see you not breaking our classroom rule about talking while others are talking. You have your hand raised and you are patiently waiting your turn. Thanks for being

so respectful.

* For a high schooler: Dorenda, you are following our classroom rule about not leaving a mess at your workstation. I see you grabbing the recycling can and making sure all your paper scraps go in there before the bell rings. You have the greatness of diligence and thoughtfulness.

To effectively work with this technique, you'll need to have clear rules for your classroom, home, or youth group setting. Many classrooms and families state their rules in "positive" language—"be respectful," "keep your hands to yourself," or "keep your bedroom neat"— and what we have found with this approach is that it's far more effective to state rules *negatively*. The line is far clearer when we state what we do NOT want:

* Instead of "be respectful"—No interrupting. No teasing. No cursing. No name calling. No leaving our seats during class time without asking.
* Instead of "keep your hands to yourself"—No pushing. No hitting. No kicking. No unwanted touching.
* Instead of "keep your bedroom neat"—No leaving a mess. No clothing on the floor. No uneaten food left in your room. No garbage on the bookshelves.

If you are required to have positively stated rules in a school setting, that's absolutely fine too; be sure to do your best with giving clear examples of what students would *not* do while following these rules. Take time to teach your rules and review them after long breaks away from school.

When creating clear rules, ask yourself what the most important things are that would benefit your classroom, home or group. Think about the fact that if these things were not happening, you would have a peaceful, pleasant and positive atmosphere for learning or enjoying family time at home. How *NOT* great would it be if those rules were being broken right now?—so, therefore, how great is it that they are currently being abided by?

Notice how many behaviors become available for recognition with this way of defining rules. If someone's not interrupting, we can call them out for that. If someone's not sticking gum under their desk, we can express our gratitude for that—especially if they have stuck gum under their desk in the past, or they have a piece of gum in their fingers and appear to be preparing to stick it under there!

That's right: you can give a Proactive Recognition to a child who seems to be on their way to breaking a rule but hasn't yet. As long as the child is not actively rule-breaking, it's time-in, and you can appreciate them for following even a rule they seem well on their way to breaking. Appreciate them with the truth of the moment.

* Roxanne, I love that you didn't retaliate with name calling even though those kids said some rough things and you could have easily lashed back at them. That reveals your have the greatness of healthy self-control and restraint. You are being that greatness.

If you are concerned that this technique will read to your students like a gilded invitation to do exactly what we don't want them to do, rest assured that they won't receive it that way—*if* the other parts of Stands One and Two are in place, and *if* (here's the biggest "if") you are *genuinely grateful* about what is *not* transpiring. If you're not coming from an undercurrent of sarcasm or snark, you'll be surprised at what happens when you explicitly appreciate a child for following the rules. And when we unfold the Third Stand more completely, you will feel well-prepared to respond effectively when a rule is broken.

SPECIFIC POINTERS FOR RULES AND ROUTINES

* Choose the top 4-6 rules you absolutely need followed to ensure a successful setting and emphasize those often through Proactive Recognition.

* Post your rules! And even if a rule has not been made explicit, it's okay to identify them on the fly, then add them to your list. "Thanks for following our rule about not bringing live animals in from the playground! That shows me that you care about keeping our classroom clean and safe for everyone." "Thanks for keeping your backpacks near the front door. You're following our rule about keeping our home organized." "Thanks for not interrupting your peers as they share. You're being so considerate right now."

* Create, teach and recognize use of clear routines for every possible action in your classroom, home and group time. This will greatly expand opportunities for Proactive Recognition; you can energize children for adhering to the routines in place, or to any aspect of those routines. For example, in a school setting, you can create routines for the following: passing papers in or out, using the restroom, phone answering, passing textbooks or novels out to classmates, getting a drink of water or sharpening a pencil, asking a question during instruction/independent practice/small group work, needing a pencil, placement of backpacks or cellphones, entering the classroom, dismissal, turning things into the office, returning play equipment, or laptop distribution. It may be useful to include class jobs as well. Post the routines and class jobs to give more possibilities for Proactive Recognitions.

If, at first, it sounds absurd to you to recognize children for not breaking rules, don't worry. This is a big shift for most people; but in the context of the overall framework of the NHA, it will come to feel perfectly sensible as you put it into practice. What's true is that boundless gratitude can be made available for the smallest gifts of positivity if we begin to look for them. Consider how *not-great* it would be right now if little Timmy unloaded a pocket full of tadpoles onto your desk! So: how great is it that he didn't bring any inside today—*especially* if he brought some inside yesterday?

As a new user of NHA, I was initially afraid to use Proactive Recognition with my middle school students. I feared that they would do exactly the thing I was recognizing them for *not* doing. I was so fearful about this that I didn't try out Proactive Recognition for an entire year — at school or at home with my own boys.

I remember the day I gave Proactive Recognition a shot at school, in a very challenging class. I figured I may as well go for it full speed ahead. I planted myself in front of a student and recognized him for looking at me while I spoke to him. "You could be telling me off, swearing in my face, tipping the desk, throwing your math book, or running out of the room." As I spoke, my fear turned into shock and then appreciation. He was taking in my recognition without diving into any of the bad behaviors I had thanked him for foregoing.

The only time I've ever had Proactive Recognition backfire is with very young children: two years old or younger. It's part of their appropriate development to try out everything they hear and see as a possibility. I didn't let these little ones' responses stop me, and I kept building the momentum I had begun, and these same children did eventually grow out of trying out what I was recognizing them for not doing as I stuck with all the techniques and stands.

— CE

Creative Recognition: This technique is designed to make success absolutely impossible to avoid—even with the most oppositional child. It involves making a specific request and then energizing the child for complying. The key here is to make requests where compliance is more or less guaranteed.

* (When child is nearly in their seat): Nico, I need you to sit down. (Pause as the child finishes sitting.) I see you in your seat before the bell. Thanks for being on time.
* (When child is about to release some trash into the wastebasket): Leo, I need you to toss your trash in the trash can. (Pause as the child completes the action.) Awesome job! Thanks for doing your part to keep the classroom tidy.
* (When you notice the child is about to clear their dinner dishes): Bryan, I need you to clear your dinner dishes. (Pause as the child completes the action.) Thanks for being so responsible and clearing your dishes.

Notice that the requests made here do not use 'polite' language like "Would you please..." or "Can you..." or "Will you..." Instead, it uses stronger, clearer language: "I need you to..." "I want you to..." or "Go ahead and..." remove the element of choice that so many challenging children will use to push every button on their favorite toy's console.

When my own boys were teenagers and I was learning the NHA, a recurring problem in our household was that no matter which son I asked to take the garbage out, the response was something along these lines: "Why are you asking me?" or "I did it yesterday!" and "Mom, it's his turn." No matter who I asked, I always got some sort of protest in response to my request. So I tried Creative Recognition.

I saw that the garbage in the kitchen needed to be emptied, and I saw that our son Jordan was nearby. I said, "Jordan, I need you to take the garbage out." He acted as if he hadn't heard a thing. Although I was having my own negative response to him ignoring me, I was able to reset, and and a minute or so later I said again, "Jordan, I need you to take the garbage out." Then I saw him stop and look at the garbage container. I quickly said, "Oh, I see you looking at it, thank you!" With a look of pure disgust, he turned and walked to the garbage while saying something like, "Okay, Mom, *geez!*" as if he were outraged. I did not react, and he quickly took the garbage out. When he came back in and started to put a new bag in the container, I recognized him for taking the trash out for me and for being so helpful.

In thinking about that interaction later on that day, I realized that I could be very impatient, and that when I asked my boys to do something I expected them to drop everything immediately and to respond to my request. I also realized that it didn't really matter if the garbage was taken out in the instant or in five minutes. What mattered most is that I made a clear request, didn't react to any negativity sent my way, and waited for the moment when I could honestly recognize any movement toward follow-through of my request.

What occurred in our home that day truly was miraculous! After that, I never once had a problem with one of my boys taking the garbage out for me. It may seem like a small thing, yet when in challenging situations with our families, our students or our clients, positive moments like these really matter.

— CE

To review: the four techniques for upholding Stand Two are about pointing out to the child:

* What IS HAPPENING that can be applauded
* What is NOT HAPPENING that can be applauded
* What this reveals about the child's greatness

While these techniques are initially taught as separate skills, this is really only for the purpose of learning many possibilities in terms of ways to notice and acknowledge a child who is not breaking rules. At the end of the day, once you build your capacity for each of them individually, you'll naturally start to use them in combination.

I have always thought of these four ways of appreciating and acknowledging as uniquely useful and purposeful in their own right — and most powerful when used in combination. I've thought of them each as a separate camera lens with its own look, angle, and movement that flow into the overall purpose of transporting a child into feeling uniquely and profoundly seen. Each lens becomes part of the bigger picture, capturing aspects that the others don't; yet, they can all combine into something even greater. In addition, the person giving the recognitions ultimately gets to see and voice the beauty they choose to speak to in their own beautiful way. You get to make this uniquely your own. At the end of the day, your personal spin, physicality, and voice will best serve to transport children into a growing sense of who they really are and reveal their true nature of greatness.

Here's an example of the way in which Nurtured Heart recognition techniques can emerge as combinations of the four you've learned, bringing to the child so much more than the sum of its parts: "Amanda, I saw that you had a flash of annoyance when I mentioned that we had homework over the weekend. I also saw a moment when you reset yourself and chose not to voice anything disruptive. Thank you for not breaking that rule. I appreciate that you have grown into having the power of restraint and self-control, and that you used great judgment and thoughtfulness to not blurt something out. That reveals your greatness of compassion and caring. I see that greatness in you."

— HG

In the next chapter, we'll take a deeper look at the Third Stand—which is designed to empower you to enhance clarity around rules and levy a predictable, non-punitive, brief consequence for rule-breaking that truly works.

I was in a sophomore high school English class leading the "Reset Before You Erupt" activity for a teacher I was coaching for behavior support and student engagement. In the past, I'd had experiences of students of all ages enjoying this activity; that day, I noticed that students appeared to be disinterested and maybe even bored.

Instead of giving up, trying to change the way I was leading or to remind students how important this activity was, I chose to reset myself and to give recognitions to any student giving me and my words even a glimmer of attention. Even when the going was rough, I continued to model strategies to raise student engagement. I was able to reset myself and to continue using the Stands often. By the time students began to create their own posters, ALL students were engaged, discussing ways to reset with each other, and marveling at the realization that they had been resetting themselves all along.

When I consider how leading this activity could have ended up with me in pure panic about students not being engaged at all to students transforming into 100% engagement before my eyes, I get chills. I'm reminded about the moments when we as parents, teachers, or youth group leaders feel momentarily panicky when things aren't going the way we expected, and that if we stick with Stands One, Two, and Three, we can actually stay on track. What a gift!

— CE

Chapter Four

THE THIRD STAND:

RESETTING OTHERS

The Third Stand, as taught to adults using the NHA in their work with youth, goes like this:

Absolutely clear! I set and enforce clear limits and consequences in an un-energized way. I always provide a true consequence when a rule is broken.

When taught to young people in GKI groups, it goes like this:

Absolutely clear! Whenever I give energy to negativity, I reset myself to seeing and acknowledging the positive. I choose to get myself back on track by resetting my words, thoughts, emotions or actions. I create my own clear rules and boundaries.

NHA brings the self-reset into the conversation as a part of Stand One. For young people, for whom it is an amazing challenge and an incredibly useful tool for managing themselves, the self-reset certainly deserves its own Stand! For adults working with children, however, it's necessary to work with, practice, and master resetting others.

As an adult authority figure, you need a reliable, congruent way to mete out non-energized consequences to the young people in your care. Without this, the first two Stands cannot work to their full potential. Like a brace you'd wear to help heal an injured back, this Approach needs all its parts to lend optimum support. If a brace is missing a connecting piece, the stability it is meant to lend is lost.

The remainder of this chapter is dedicated to this type of reset. Throughout the Greatness Kids Initiative, the self-reset as Stand Three is taught and reinforced, and that angle will become clearer and more practical for you as well as you work through the activities.

One high school student beautifully encapsulated the distinction between *being* reset by someone else and resetting himself. He raised his hand during an activity and said, "So a reset is...we make a mistake, we *get* a reset, OR we think in our head, 'Oh, wait, I'm at school and I can't do that here—I need to follow the school rules,' and then I *do* follow the rules...and you're saying I've reset *myself*?"
Exactly.
— CE

YOU KNOW YOU'RE READY TO DEEPEN YOUR PRACTICE OF RESETTING OTHERS WHEN:

1. You have firmly established your own ability to reset yourself, and practice self-resets often—ideally, doing so transparently in front of others at least some of the time.

2. You have clearly established rules, stated in negative language ("No hitting, no cursing, no speaking when someone else is speaking..."). You have a strong and dedicated practice of using Stand Two recognitions.

This story from Celeste illustrates the ways in which Stand One and Stand Three resets differ and work in tandem:

I was teaching one of the most challenging groups of middle school students I've ever worked with in an alternative education setting. On this particular day, I was struggling with the behavior in the class and was also struggling with being able to fully reset myself.

I walked over to a student to offer a reset practically in their face. With gritted teeth and a voice full of anger, I said, *"I need you to reset RIGHT NOW."* As soon as I'd spoken, I recognized that I needed to reset myself immediately.

I stood tall, took a deep breath or two. Knowing that all the students were watching carefully, I announced that I actually needed to reset myself. I then bent toward the student I was so angry with and said, "I apologize for the way I just spoke to you. I am reset now. I see that you are too, thank you." I was then able to move on with teaching and the initial disturbance ended. No follow-up discussion was needed about the student's behavior or mine. It was over and in the past.

— CE

WHAT IS THE RESET? —

The reset, in this context, is a pause in engagement from you—the child's favorite toy—following the breaking of a rule. It is given as the consequence of that rule-breaking.

A reset can be as brief as a couple of seconds or as long as a minute or two, but should not be longer than this (think Video Game logic; you want to get the child back into time-in as quickly as possible).

Reset is non-punitive, brief, and completely free of emotional charge.

A reset can end as soon as the child stops breaking the rule. As soon as the rule-breaking has ceased, you can find something to energize/recognize (Stand Two), and then call the reset over.

Giving a reset looks like this:

1. **Say the child's name, followed by "Reset."** Be careful to give the word as little mojo as possible. There should be no emotional charge around resetting; it's nothing more than a pause and a chance to make a better choice.

2. **Unplug your energy from the child.** Turn away—not in an emotionally activated way, but in a way that kindly expresses your unavailability for connection around the rule that has just been broken. Think in terms of 'unplugging' or any other imagery that helps you feel this with clarity.

3. **Refrain from any kind of explanation about why the reset is happening,** including telling the child what they've done wrong. This will be revealed in the welcome-back restoration following the reset (essentially, a Proactive Recognition), once the child is no longer doing whatever got them into reset in the first place.

4. **Stay tuned in enough to the child, peripherally, to notice any shift away from the unwanted behavior and into something new that's positive or neutral.** Allow yourself to deeply and heartfully perceive what is transpiring in these moments.

5. **As soon as you see a success to acknowledge, jump in; acknowledge the child's success; and welcome them back from the reset in some way that lets them know they've completed it.** Even if the child has only seemed to pause in the rule-breaking behavior, grab that moment and acknowledge it. "Lamara, right now, you aren't cursing at me. I can see you're still angry, so I know that this is requiring great self-control. Thanks for resetting."

6. **It may be that the child will jump right back into the unwanted behavior, especially if they are testing the new normal and trying to get you to revert to the old way of doing things.** If that happens, simply reset them again. You might have to do this several times in a row. It's okay. Each reset is a new beginning.

THE TWO-DOLLAR SPEEDING TICKET

This is a story Howard uses to illustrate how the reset—an un-energized, brief, non-punitive consequence—can work to shift even the most challenging behaviors:

Imagine you have a habit of driving 50 in a 35 mph zone. One day, you get pulled over, much to your chagrin. The officer is courteous and calm, writes you a ticket, and hands it to you, saying "Have a nice day." You look at the ticket. What?! It's only for two dollars. No big deal at all! You zoom off at your usual 50 mph.

But this keeps on happening. Every day, you speed, and every day, you get a two-dollar speeding ticket. This officer never seems to miss your law-breaking choice. It's making you late for appointments and this is starting to become an irritation.

Some of us would just slow down or try a different route. Maybe you're not one of those kinds of people. If you're intense, maybe you apply your considerable energies to outsmarting the cop or talking them out of giving you the ticket. No matter what you do—no matter your pleading, flirting, joking, veiled threats, or passive-aggressive jabs—It's always the same routine: pull over, ticket through the window, and "Have a nice day."

The cop's refusal to engage with you beyond this allows you to have a pure experience of the consequence. Eventually—perhaps after even more escalation—you decide it's no longer worth it. It becomes increasingly boring and frustrating, and eventually, it's the fuel of those very emotions that lead you to a new decision. You start to apply your intensity to driving 35 or slower on this road.

In the *Transforming the Intense Child Workbook*, Howard concludes:

The child may need a hundred $2 speeding tickets to get with the new program, or he may need ten thousand. Either way, your job is the same. Keep resetting yourself. Refuse to escalate, lecture, cajole, or otherwise push the issue (Stand One). Get out of the way and let the child figure it out for himself. Give simple, unceremonious resets (Stand One). Let him develop the internal motivation to shift. Trust that connection with you, with ever-better positive bandwidth (Stand Two), is his ultimate goal; and that he will eventually choose the path that most reliably yields that connection. (p. 93)

Work diligently to get out of the way of the child experiencing the reset purely. Any time you fall away from maintaining Stand One, reset yourself and try again. Continue to provide evidence through consistent resets and high-powered appreciations that this new path is impossible to avoid, and that you won't be deterred along it—no matter what. Come back to total clarity about whether rules are being followed or broken and stay in the present moment and all its gifts.

Don't warn a child, "I'm going to reset you if…"! Warnings, though compassionately intended, will get in the way by giving the gift of you though negativity, and by sending the message that the rules don't have to be taken seriously. A little bit of a broken rule is still a broken rule. This simple and unceremonious reset relieves you of any need to provide warnings. Rule broken, even the tiniest bit? Reset.

INTRODUCING THE RESET TO CHILDREN IN YOUR CARE

Preschoolers through third graders tend to get the logic of the reset without any explanation. You can simply begin to give them and watch the magic unfold.

Older children might have a greater need for this form of consequence to be explained. You can do so using words like the following: "I've decided that I don't want to be punishing or lecturing anymore. That's a real drag for you and for me, especially now that I am staying focused on all you are doing to follow our rules and contribute positively. From now on, if you do break a rule, I'm just going to say 'Reset,' and then you'll have a chance to make a different choice. When you do, I'm going to recognize you for that! I'm loving how it feels to keep this simple and move through problems quickly... and I know you'll get used to it soon enough."

Sometimes, a child's acting-out seems to rise from deep emotional distress, fatigue, or from not feeling well. This may bring up a powerful urge in you to comfort and care-give in those moments, rather than delivering the needed reset and briefly turning away. It's crucial, especially at these times, that you stick to this low-key, utterly consistent, simple reset.

One key strategy to use when a child is acting out and rule-breaking out of frustration, anxiety, anger, or other heightened emotions is to energize every aspect you can see of their attempts to manage their own emotions and complete the task at hand. Be certain to only give this appreciative recognition when the rules have not been broken, or after the reset—when they still are in that intensity, but are no longer acting out.

I had been working with the NHA for a year or so when my then-three-year-old son Noah threw a tantrum at a music performance. It had been a long day; he had been sick; and it was just too much for him to sit still and listen to the music in a room full of grownups.

I reset him and with no emotional energy carried him outside. As he screamed his head off but held my hand and walked alongside me down the sidewalk, I remained calm on the outside (although inside, every molecule of my being wanted to just cuddle, hold, and comfort my exhausted, falling-apart baby boy).

Every time he took a breath between yells, I energized him for remembering to take deep breaths and for feeling his big feelings and working so hard to calm himself down. I energized him for holding my hand and walking with me even though he was so upset. Within minutes, he had stopped crying. He turned his tear-stained face up to me and said proudly, "Mommy! I calmed myself down!"

— ML

Where adults establish a pattern of giving themselves fully to the child when they are at some stage of tantruming, the child learns that this is a reliable way to extract adult connection and will be prone to going back to that again and again—especially at times where their need for relationship is high. While this might recall that old notion that an emotionally unhinged child is "just trying to get attention" and should be ignored, this is a much more nuanced way of working with children in the throes of emotional upset. This is a strategy led to Noah feeling empowered, even at the tender age of three, in managing his emotions.

Yes: a child who is acting out of challenging emotions IS trying to get attention—and that is exactly what is most natural and healthy for a child to be doing. Their actions are designed, from day one, to get adults to tend to and care for them. We aren't sure when or how that started to be a negative thing; it's just human development in action.

Children try all kinds of things to get us connected and engaged and they will continue to do the things that bring that fastest, most powerfully and most reliably, especially if they possess strong intensity and life-force. We get to decide what those things are: helplessness and distress, or the child successfully finding a better way through moments of helplessness and distress.

The trick is to show the child that being emotionally unhinged is not the best way to get adults to show up with high-intensity love, relationship and care. We can certainly hold the child in our hearts with compassion and empathy, because we all know how hard it can be to follow the rules of life when we're feeling sick or are overwhelmed with emotions like anger or fear—especially if we are naturally intense. But we do them the most good when we give the reset regardless of the child's state of sickness or emotionality. This is what will ultimately come around to build the child's resilience and self-reliance.

This being said, safety is absolutely the first priority. If a child is a danger to self or others, do what's needed to restore safety, even if that means temporarily abandoning Stands One and Three. Return to the Stands as soon as possible.

While I was leading a Greatness Intervention group with 7th and 8th graders, two students became intensely upset with each other, stood up, began yelling, and then started to fight physically. This all happened in a matter of seconds. The rest of us stopped the activity, and the other students watched in disbelief and waited with some excitement to see how I would handle the situation. I'm not sure of what I did exactly; I know for a fact that I approached the students who were fighting with the intention of them stopping, and that I gave as little energy (reaction, response, energy, relationship) to them as possible. They stopped quickly, and as soon as they were able to take a breath and calm down, I sent them one at a time to the office — which happened to be just outside of our door. Without saying a word to the class, I made a call to the assistant principal to let him know what had happened. I spoke calmly and thanked him for supporting the students. I remember the next moments in slow motion. As I turned toward the students, I saw a look of intrigue cross their faces. I could feel their anticipation of a big discussion or lecture about what had just happened. I took in their energy and used it to force myself to get back on track with the lesson...*without saying a word about the fight.* When a student tried to start up a conversation about the fight, I simply reset the group and moved on with my lesson. We were able to continue without a hitch.

DOES USING RESETS MEAN KIDS "GET AWAY" WITH BAD BEHAVIOR? —

Some adults cringe at the idea that a child doing serious harm could get away with just an un-energized reset. This is understandable! If you need to mandate some form of restoration or repair in order to have completion around an incident of rule-breaking, this Approach allows for this; just be sure that you move forward with plans for this in adherence to the Stands, and give lots of Stand Two recognitions for every step the child takes toward beginning or completing that restoration or repair. Broach the topic of repair after resets are complete and you are back in appreciation mode with the child and some time has passed. Enlist the child's input on what they think a suitable repair/restoration might look like. This addition is best reserved for when something or someone is broken or hurt.

A much more complete treatment of resetting others can be found in the *Transforming the Intense Child Workbook,* pages 85-106.

Over the years while practicing the Three Stands of the NHA in classrooms, in small groups, and in my home, I sometimes found myself using the Three Stands as a way to control a situation. I may have been attempting to control events, outcomes, or behaviors, but overall, the realization that mattered was that if I am wanting to control, the energy may be felt by children—and my effectiveness is decreased.

Where I behave through the lens of wanting to control, I operate through my head and not my heart. Howie will sometimes joke, "This is not called the Nurtured Head Approach," and this is a gentle way to remember that we are most effective when we surrender a need to control and return to the heart's imperative: love.

Surrender here looks like being able to use the Three Stands in concert, with trust and confidence, even when my head is saying, "It may not work this time!" I can never predict the next *now,* but I can trust that I have excellent tools at my disposal—ones I have seen, felt, and experienced as making a positive difference.

—CE

Chapter Five

THE GIFT OF "BEING THE NHA"

AS THE ACTIVITIES LEADER

In a Greatness Kids Initiative group for sixth through eighth graders, Celeste had a new eighth grade girl—Allie—join. She was new to the school and entered the group well after mid-year norms, routines, and expectations had been well-established.

The first day, Allie loudly directed inappropriate comments at her peers and to Celeste as group leader. She ran and slid her entire body headfirst across an eight-foot-long table, as though she were on a slip-n-slide.

Celeste used the Three Stands with her and with her peers. She recognized the other group members for not giving attention to her behaviors; for choosing not to yell at her or to respond to negative comments addressed to them.

On the second day, they didn't see any more table sliding. Celeste continued to use the Three Stands. Still, Allie made many more inappropriate comments to her peers and to Celeste. The rest of the class continued to do well with not giving her negative behavior their energy.

Through most of the first couple of weeks, the negative comments continued, along with negative behaviors: clearing off a table with a broad sweep of her arm, throwing a container of pencils on the floor, knocking a phone off of a table.

What do you suppose Celeste did? Yes: she continued with consistent use of the Three Stands, in particular providing her with clear, targeted recognitions (Baby Steps) as often as possible. It appeared that Allie didn't quite know what to make of it, but this really got her attention.

As Allie realized that Celeste saw her only for her good behaviors and made the connection that this good part of her was actually her real, true self, a terrible cycle began to be broken. As her first couple of weeks with the group ended, Allie was sitting appropriately at the table. She appeared to be working to fit in—participating and willing to be reset, and to accept recognitions.

About a month into Allie's time with the group, they were doing an activity that involved intensively energizing/recognizing a classmate for 30 seconds (1:1 Energizing). This was when Celeste saw Allie shift from an expectation of being 'seen' most vividly when acting out to one of being seen and acknowledged for the ways she was successful.

As she was recognized by her peer, Allie's body language changed: she went from being poised to protest to what looked like a state of pure listening and acceptance. As Allie's peer gave her a recognition for looking pretty, her eyes filled with tears. She turned to Celeste and said, "No one has ever said that to me."

Once both Allie and her partner had finished giving their recognitions, Celeste gave laser-focused recognitions to both of them. Allie took them in completely. After group time, Celeste called Allie over once more to zero in on more recognitions for her: for her maturity, her ability to accept recognitions, her positive choices to follow the rules of the activity, and so on. Celeste gave her absolute attention and purely positive relationship; she accepted it fully.

Allie entered into strongly positive, honest, and trustworthy relationships in her GKI group. The positive behaviors she had come to express in group began to show up throughout her school day. She appeared happy and content with who she was, and she no longer needed to use negative behaviors to get peer and adult attention.

During a guest observation near the end of the school year, Allie showed tremendous growth. She was a positive participant who enjoyed lots of positive interactions; she had grown comfortable with being herself. Her Inner Wealth was growing.

What enabled Celeste to get through the initial struggles with Allie, and to support her movement into a new way of being and relating, was her own commitment. She was not about to let this child derail her. She was fiercely determined, and her determination gave the other students in the group permission to be equally determined. Together, they created a powerful and safe space where Allie could transform herself.

This is what we call "*being* the Approach."

The Nurtured Heart Approach itself has been built and refined to transform relationships. It was born out of work with the most challenging children and just so happened to work for the classmates and siblings of these children as well. If the Stands are followed and the techniques used properly and consistently, create positive change will happen.

What takes the Approach to the next level of impact—transforming a kid as tough as Allie in the space of a month—is the focus, intention, and determination of the adult who is leading the shift. Role modeling a fierce, warrior-like, fearless, and relentless application of the Approach is the main ingredient for transformed relationships—the kind that build both improved behavior and Inner Wealth.

Ferocity? Warrior energy? Relentlessness? Fearlessness? These notions run counter to many folks' first impression of the Nurtured Heart Approach as a soft, fluffy love-fest. This approach is decidedly *not* that. Using the NHA takes dedication, determination, accountability and practice, and if we don't bring our own intensity to the game, we hamstring our own chances of having maximum impact.

To those who have laughed at and made fun of this Approach, describing it as over-positive, or silly, or [insert whatever derogatory descriptives you've heard], we say this: The importance of building inner wealth in our youth today is no laughing matter. We *must* do what we can to make children feel seen; to teach them that they *do* matter and that they are valuable human beings. We need to take this commitment on in our homes, in our schools, and in any youth group setting we can, in order to change the negative behaviors happening in our culture. There is no time to waste. The moment is now. We need to show kids their greatness and to love them for who they really are!

What does it feel like to be in this warrior mode? The best way we can describe it is that we're seeing nothing but the child we are speaking to in the moment. We are 100 percent present and honed in on the child completely, in a total flow with that child. We click into a deep state of connection; our heart gains access to seeing and speaking to the true beauty of this human being in front of us.

Time slows down. The child's qualities of greatness light up brightly, moving to the forefront of my awareness; negativity fades into the background, lacking even a fraction of the strength required to cast its shadow on that greatness.

These moments are the greatest joys of our work and of our lives. Getting to this place takes time and practice, and it's the most worthwhile place we've ever been. It begins with total commitment to not only "doing" the NHA, but to *being* the NHA.

When you begin to step into this mode, it starts to impact you well beyond work with the children in your life. It becomes a potent internal practice.

I picked up cards from a friend for a presentation the next morning; her three-year-old daughter was the one who handed them to me. As I drove home, I stopped at a light, in a city where the camera takes a picture of you if you run a red light. It's a $500 ticket if you get nailed this way.

Sitting in the left-hand turn lane at the red light, I thought, *I should have counted the cards!* I pulled them out and quickly counted them, then noticed the light had turned green, and went for it. As I went through the intersection, the light turned yellow, and I saw a big flash.

I was *livid!* I was going to have to pay a huge fine *and* complete traffic school. I hadn't really done anything wrong; I hadn't been speeding or trying to run the red light! I spent some time being angry at the system, and then some more time being angry at myself…then, I took some deep breaths and said to myself: "There's nothing I can do to change this. I'm not going to let this ruin my night, or any more of the month it will take for me to get the ticket in the mail." I then took that powerful energy deep into my heart and used it to send all my cells the message: *I am the greatness of incredible restraint and of letting go.* By the time I'd gotten home, I had reset myself pretty much completely.

Turned out, I didn't get a ticket. The light had flashed at someone else. I could've wasted weeks worrying and being mad at myself over this. Instead, I chose to reset: to let go of the story I didn't want to tell…and it turned out to not even be true.

How often do we experience stress, anxiety, or even anguish around negative stories? This is an opportunity to notice this habit and to choose a reset instead.

— CE

This can be a hard sell for some people. It's one thing to adopt an approach and use it to try to manage a classroom or a challenging child. It's quite another to shift your entire mindset—to (not really, but in effect) 'police' yourself, self-correct away from negativity, and overall to live your life in a way dictated by some approach designed by a therapist in Tucson who you may or may not have ever met or heard of before you picked up this book.

If this feels like a stretch to you, you're not alone. And if you want to have maximum impact in your GKI groups, this is how you do it.

The good news about this is that "being the NHA" is a pretty sure route to being grateful, mindful, and happy. It re-wires a very powerful and deeply entrenched bias toward negativity (more on this below).

REWIRING THE BRAIN FOR POSITIVITY

In effect...the brain is like Velcro for negative experiences but Teflon for positive ones...To keep our ancestors alive, Mother Nature evolved a brain that routinely tricked them into making three mistakes: overestimating threats, underestimating opportunities, and underestimating resources (for dealing with threats and fulfilling opportunities). This is a great way to pass on gene copies, but a lousy way to promote quality of life.

—Rick Hanson, PhD, psychologist, author, and positivity researcher

Human beings are wired to look for problems and danger. This is why, when we walk into a room, even the smallest negative factor stands out, and why we tend to overlook the many positive and neutral factors present in the same room at the same time.

In psychology, this is called "negativity bias"—and it's not just a habit: it's built into our brains. The Nurtured Heart Approach works, in large part, by training our brains to express a *positivity* bias: by making a habit of resetting ourselves away from negative perceptions and expressions and choosing to perceive and express what's going well or that isn't *not* going well.

Remember Allie from the beginning of this chapter? Consider the response she was used to getting by the time she walked into our GKI group. Even minor negative behaviors, far less significant than table-sliding and disrespectful language, had typically been handled by removing her from the class, giving a punishment, assigning her with community service, or taking away a privilege. At some point, she started making the choice to go down the road of negativity, and the way adults responded to her ended up not dissuading those behaviors but reinforcing them. And these initial adult attempts to stop Allie from breaking rules came from a negativity bias: see the problem, troubleshoot the problem, try anything and everything to solve the problem. These well-intended choices only served to support Allie's movement deeper into the cycle of negativity as she received more and more attention and relationship for negative behaviors.

Rick Hanson, PhD advises us to "be mindful of the degree to which your brain is wired to make you afraid...and to zero in on any apparent bad news in a larger stream of information...to tune out or de-emphasize reassuring good news, and to keep thinking about the one thing that was negative in a day in which a hundred small things happened, ninety-nine of which were neutral or positive."

This is what we do as we first develop Stand One (Absolutely no energy to negativity). First implementing this Stand can feel like rolling a giant boulder uphill! Moment after moment after moment, we are confronted with our own negativity biases, and asked to choose—*every time*—to give our energy to something positive (Stand Two). Sticking with that alone requires some warrior energy! Add to this that when working on Stand One while leading a youth group there are actually two things going on: we are working to avoid giving attention/relationship to negative behaviors as they pop up... AND we are battling our own negative thoughts about those behaviors. This is a challenge worthy of a warrior.

When your intention is to lead GKI groups, your commitment to this warrior-like adherence to the NHA will be contagious. As you know well if you're an educator or have other experience working with or parenting youth, children are more profoundly impacted by what we DO than what we SAY; by WHO WE ARE and HOW WE SHOW UP than by what we say we believe or think is best.

Lived values are much more powerful than ones paid lip service—even when that lip service is as eloquent as lip service has ever been. Passionately lived values are more powerful yet.

Take this understanding with you as you move further into the "how" of bringing the GKI to groups of youth. Once you feel that incredible feeling described earlier—that profound, highly energized connection between you and the kid that everyone said no one could handle—and when you see a kid who might have ended up in the worst kind of trouble coming to a place of thriving and shining out greatness...our guess is that you'll be ready to call yourself a NHA warrior, too.

Chapter Six

GREATNESS KIDS

INITIATIVE ACTIVITIES

Each of the activity plans in this chapter is designed to take place in a 30-minute time slot. They are meant to be brought to a GKI group in the order listed here. In chapters to come, you'll find many other options for GKI activities that you can introduce after building a Nurtured Heart foundation with these initial plans.

Throughout all activities, remember to:

* Make passing an option during circle or group sharing. Give zero energy to that option when chosen while energizing those choosing to participate during the activity.
* Remind the group about their confidentiality agreement (which they will make during the first activity) when you or students are sharing personal stories or stories that need to remain confidential.
* Use resets from day one as needed! Model resetting yourself in front of your group when possible, and use humor while modeling resetting yourself or sharing your own examples of resetting.
* Be sure to take necessary steps to connect students with support when/if they share information regarding self-harm and/or the harm of others.

Begin your GKI groups with this introductory day.

* Begin by introducing yourself and your intention for leading your group. Your intention should be different from the purpose of GKI. For example: "The purpose of Greatness Kids Initiative is to have children explore how to use the Nurtured Heart Approach on themselves. My intention is to provide the tools for you to live out the greatness you have inside you, and to teach you some strategies that will help you be a great friend and classmate who feels great about yourself and appreciates other people."
* Invite students to introduce themselves to the whole group by stating their name/grade level. Share that you will be supporting them in using the Nurtured Heart Approach in their own lives and that you will use NHA as you teach.
* Explain the overall purpose of NHA, including the building of inner wealth. Explain to youth what it means to build inner wealth; you may find it useful to use the idea of the "portfolio" (page 33) as a way to teach this message.
* Discuss the importance of confidentiality. Explain that if a student shares ideas of self-harm or harming others, you will take steps to connect them with appropriate support. Ask the group to agree verbally to confidentiality.
* Create or share group expectations/norms/rules. Clear rules for groups may be created ahead of time and posted from the very first meeting or can be brainstormed and written up with the group if time permits. Rules could consist of: No inappropriate language, No being out of seat without permission, No calling out. Choose rules that are simple, clear and meaningful for your group.
* Give students a chance to ask questions.
* End group time with appreciations of the entire group and their participation. If any students appear to be apprehensive about being in the group or about the verbal confidentiality agreement, energize them for their caution, insightfulness, and awareness. Ask them to agree to participate for at least the first two meetings. Usually a one-on-one conversation is enough to manage their concerns and persuade them to enroll.

* Model using the approach starting NOW. Use genuine recognitions often.

> Edward was a member of a high school Greatness Kids group. Following a discussion about Inner Wealth, he shared that he already has a sense of seeing what's irrelevant in his life. He went on about not needing NHA Greatness Kids and said, "no offense, but it's a waste of my time." He said he was already there.
>
> I listened and told him I could see he really did have a high level of knowing his own strengths and strong self-control. I also told him that even though he already got it, I totally valued his input and comments during our group time. He didn't complain after this point and went on to participate fully as a valued part of our group.
> — CE

INNER WEALTH

This activity serves to introduce participants to the concept of Inner Wealth, using a scene from the film *The Horse Whisperer* as a starting point.[4] To prepare, cue up *The Horse Whisperer* riding scene on youtube.com (https://www.youtube.com/watch?v=KjcUBcdERhI), and keep a whiteboard and whiteboard marker on hand.

* Introduce the term "inner wealth" and have students brainstorm its meaning.
* After brainstorming, share a broad definition of inner wealth: Inner wealth is what we all believe to be true about ourselves and whatever language we may use to define it.
* Talk about why kids need to be strong on the inside. Have students share out their opinions on this. Be sure to discuss the pressures of being a child and a student today.

---

[4]A synopsis: teenager Grace is injured and traumatized in a riding accident that also seriously injures her horse. Grace is despondent; her new anthem in life is 'I can't,' and she resists her mom's attempts to help. Her mother, a high-powered magazine editor, recognizes that she will need to take Grace and her horse to a "horse whisperer" named Tom Booker, knowing that if the horse can heal, her daughter will too. The scene used here shows Grace confronting her fears around her first time riding again since the accident.

* Give the background of *The Horse Whisperer* movie and show the video clip.
* Discuss the young girl's level of inner wealth at the start of the clip.
* Have students name the positive qualities they see the young girl demonstrating as she chooses to approach the horse, gives him love and attention, and then rides him without giving up. List comments on the whiteboard.
* Guide students to a recognition that every single day, they are successful in many ways that might go unnoticed.
* Close the session by giving positive recognitions to students, using Baby Steps to highlight even the smallest successes. (There is no need to teach Baby Steps at this point. You are simply modeling what Robert Redford was doing in the video clip.)
* Strategically use recognitions to make the point about 'it's not a matter of whether you can or can't, you are' about whatever you are acknowledging.

ENERGY AND INTENSITY

For this activity, cue up *Toddler Throwing a Funny Tantrum:* https://www.youtube.com/watch?v=Gk-OfmmRaqs

* Go around the circle (group) and ask individual students to share when they get the most energy (attention) from their teachers, peers and/or parents. Is it when things are going well, or when things are not so great?
* Show the video clip.
* Go around the circle once again and ask students to share what they think was going on in the video.
* Ask students whether they have young children in their lives. Ask them whether they have examples of their own to share that echo the message of the video.
* Lead students to the topics of energy and the intensity of the baby and also of the mom and the dog.
* Be sure to discuss the fact that the video demonstrates classic ignoring.
* Next, ask students to randomly share what happens when they don't get desired attention when they are upset. How do they feel?
* Close by sharing that you (the teacher/leader) choose to give attention to

others when things are going well. Ask whether they have noticed this already in the way you interact with them.

BABY STEPS

For this activity, cue up the video *Be Grateful & Learn to Appreciate the Small Things in Life: It's A Beautiful Day and I Can't See It!*: https://www.youtube.com/watch?v=mj6cRdlUiJU

* Introduce the concept of Baby Steps.
* Give examples of Baby Steps from your own life.
* Show the video clip.
* Ask for feedback about the video. Why did the new language on the sign make a difference? Discuss the power of seeing what's going well even when everything appears to be going wrong.
* Review the idea that only WE can choose what we give our attention to every day and in every moment.
* Ask students to share things from their own lives that they are grateful for in this moment. Be sure to allow students to pass if you choose to go around the circle for sharing.
* Close with positive recognitions for participation, honesty, openness, and any other positive qualities you have seen today throughout the group. Point out even the smallest successes to support the concept of Baby Steps.

If students appear to be struggling with the idea of Baby Steps, try using this analogy: When growing a vegetable garden, gardeners typically notice, appreciate and celebrate the blossoms as they appear on their vegetable plants, and then begin to appreciate the tiny vegetables forming on the plants. Gardeners don't begin to be appreciative of the vegetables they grow only as they pick the ripe veggie! They are aware of and appreciate the entire process.

While presenting the idea of Baby Steps in a GKI group in Juvenile Hall, I was focusing specifically on how to appreciate even the smallest things in our lives. The first reactions to my activity (sharing what was appreciated in the moment) were related to not being able to see anything good in the JDF setting. The students began to chime in with the notion that it would be much easier to list out everything that was wrong in their current living situation.

I recognized them for their statements and their honesty while continuing to encourage them to see things they could be grateful for, even when so much seemed wrong. I remember a student sharing that he was grateful to have food to eat. After that share, a whole new level of gratitude opened up for the students. They were able to dig deep, past what they saw as wrong, and to appreciate what was right. They shared comments including:

I'm alive

I'm healthy

I get food

I'm warm

I'm safe

I have a roof over my head

I get to go to school

I get to breathe fresh air during physical education

I can earn my high school credits

I'm in a place away from temptation

I'm getting clean

I feel better

— CE

QUALITIES OF GREATNESS

For this lesson, cue up the Nick Vujicic video titled *LOOK AT YOURSELF AFTER WATCHING THIS.mp4*: https://www.youtube.com/watch?v=Gc4HGQHgeFE ...or any video that could be useful in teaching students how to name positive qualities in the face of challenges.

* Show the Nick Vujicic video.
* Answer any questions about the video or Nick's disability. He was born without limbs, and his doctors have never found any explanation for his condition.
* Ask students if they were surprised by the things Nick can do. Share that he has chosen not to be limited in his life. Let students know that he drives a boat, can swim, has a family, plays soccer, uses a diving board, and travels around the world to do motivational speaking presentations.
* Introduce the idea that Nick possesses many positive qualities.
* Write the title "Nick's Qualities of Greatness" on the whiteboard, and then go around the circle one at a time to give students the opportunity to share what they see as a quality of greatness in Nick. Write the list on the board; contribute your own suggestions as needed.
* If time allows, give students the opportunity to go around the room and name a quality of greatness they see in themselves. (This should come easily, as you—the trainer/leader—have been pointing out their qualities of greatness in every group meeting.)
* Finish by pointing out positive qualities you see in your students.

VIDEO GAME THEORY —

This activity will support you in introducing Video Game Theory to GKI groups.

* Challenge youth to think about pinpointing exactly what it is about video games that they love. Ask for a few ideas.
* Brainstorm the most popular or favorite video games. Make a list of all the things they say they enjoy about these games.
* If youth start to share about actual video game experiences, stay alert to those that can be woven into the teachings of this activity.
* Brainstorm and discuss with youth what exactly it is about video games that they love. Help them arrive at a recognition of their *clarity* and *predictability*. Help them to recognize that real life is not often clear and predictable, and that your goal as a leader of GKI is to make the time together as fun and engaging as the video games they love—to create a space where real life CAN feel as clear and predictable as video games do.
* As an example, help students recall a recent reset given in the classroom,

and help them see how this is like a video game: that you, the group leader, always provide a fresh start that brings them right back into the action following a consequence.

* Explain that video games are never too tired to give a reward or a consequence.
* Introduce the idea that video games are an example of energy being exchanged, just like energy is exchanged between people.
* Give an example of meeting someone and feeling their negative energy. Describe how you can feel that energy, and ask the group whether anyone has any comments or experiences with this kind of energy. Ask students to think of someone in their life whose energy has been positive, and where a positive relationship was created around that energy. Give students the opportunity to share.
* Close by reiterating how the Nurtured Heart Approach is like a video game: it supports people like you (the group leader) in giving attention and relationship when things are going well, and to give little energy and clear consequences when things are not going well or a rule is broken.

NHA'S THREE STANDS

This activity will support you in introducing the Three Stands to youth.

* Set yourself up to make a three-column chart with brainstormed ideas for each of the Three Stands as part of this lesson. You may choose to prepare the chart ahead of time with the headings: Stand One, Absolutely No; Stand Two, Absolutely Yes; and Stand Three, Absolute Clarity.
* Point out the GKI Three Stands on your whiteboard and describe them in detail: zero energy to negativity, seeing qualities of greatness in ourselves and others, and resetting ourselves. Talk about what it means to take a stand and include input from students. Note the simplicity of The Three Stands.
* Invite students to focus on Stand One. Brainstorm and discuss what not energizing negativity could mean for students in the group. Lead them to ideas like: not sharing gossip, choosing not to bully, not giving energy to negative states like worry or doubt, and not participating with classmates in negative behaviors. List ideas in the first column of the whiteboard.
* Invite students to focus on Stand Two. Brainstorm and have a discussion

related to what seeing the qualities of greatness in others could mean for students in the group. Lead them to ideas like making kind comments, thanking a teacher, saying hello to a peer who appears to be lonely, and noticing the (positive) little things about friends and letting them know you appreciate them. List ideas in the second column on the whiteboard.

* Invite students to focus on Stand Three. Explain that the approach was first created for adults to use with their children and students (if you haven't already). Talk about the fact that a consequence is simply what follows a broken rule or negative behavior that crosses a line and in the world at large that it could include: a punishment, ignoring, community service, loss of a privilege, or—in the case of The Nurtured Heart Approach—a reset. By this time, group leaders have been using resets in the group and hopefully resetting themselves in front of the students.

* Brainstorm specific reasons a student or an adult could be reset and/or specific reasons they could reset themselves. List reasons for resetting ourselves in the third column on the whiteboard.

* Talk through a few examples of self-resets that students might try: for example, if a student wants to get out of their seat, starts to get up, doesn't, and chooses to follow the rules by raising their hand and asking the teacher for permission, they have reset themselves.

* Discuss the idea that we all can choose to reset our thoughts, our words and/or our actions. Share experiences of resetting yourself as an adult and explain the value of the skill of resetting yourself.

* Appreciate your group either individually or as a whole for their participation and contributions and whatever else you are grateful for. Allow your heart to have a voice.

GREATNESS CHAIN ⚊

This activity is all about everyone encouraging others' successes. I have seen as many as 24 students complete it successfully. If you have a very large group, you may want to have two games going on with fewer participants in each, but don't be afraid to let a large group take this on!

* Seat students in a circle or oval so that all participants are able to see each other.
* One student will begin the activity by stating a quality of their own

greatness and evidence of the quality they've chosen. For example: "I am artistic, and I paint every weekend," or "I am helpful, and I babysit my little brother each afternoon."

* The student to the right of the first student will repeat what the first student said and will then state their own quality of greatness and evidence to support it. For example: "You are artistic, and you paint every weekend…and I am honest, because I never tell a lie."

* The activity continues on with each new participant to the right, each having the challenge of repeating what every player ahead of them has said.

* The goal is to get all the way around the circle with everyone being able to repeat what all of their peers have said before them.

* Have some ideas in mind to support success during this lesson, which requires strong memory and attentive listening. These could include options for asking a group member for help: for example, allowing students to request a clue when they can't remember the qualities shared by another participant. With younger participants, the leader may choose to have the next person repeat only what the last participant shared.

Gabriella was a participant in a class-wide high school Greatness Kids group. One day during group time, she expressed her dislike of me and what I was teaching. In particular, she talked about hating hearing the word "reset." She said she wanted to scream at me every time she heard it.

I listened to her with 100% attention, told her she got it, recognized her for not yelling, and went on with the lesson. After it was over, I overheard Gabriella launching into a profanity-laden rant about me. On my way out, I went to Gabriella and let her know how much I appreciated having a girl in the group (she was the only one at that time), how much I valued her input even though she was annoyed with the subject matter, and how beautiful she was, inside and out

As Gabriella listened, her anger seemed to vanish. She moved closer, reached out and touched my necklace and told me how much she liked it. From then on, Gabriella and I had a positive relationship with trust that it was okay for her to say how she was truly feeling.

— CE

RESETS —

For this activity, cue up *E:60 Simone Biles - Rio Olympics 2016* video clip: https://www.youtube.com/watch?v=beYj01OX3E8. Also have some sticky notes on hand.

* Open with the idea that "resetting" is just an alternate term for something everyone already does on a regular basis. Introduce the idea that athletes must learn how to reset themselves after every mistake, or they would never be successful. Mention examples like a quarterback being sacked three times in a row and not giving up; a dancer falling down, then getting back up to complete her dance; or a pitcher continuing to throw great pitches after giving up a home run.
* Show the video clip about Simone Biles.
* Ask the group to brainstorm about different times in Simone's life where she could have given up. Discuss her mindset around decisions she had to make.
* Point out that resets can range from choosing to stop tapping a pencil to taking responsibility after offending someone.
* If time allows, have students write things they could reset themselves about on sticky notes. Place the notes in like groups on the whiteboard. Students will be able to see common reasons for self-resetting, and to recognize that resets have a wide range of applications.
* Share your own stories of situations where you have chosen to reset yourself.
* Ask students if they would be willing to share their own stories of resetting themselves in their own lives.
* Be sure to include a discussion reflecting that a reset is not a punishment. Find a spot in your lesson where this concept fits naturally.
* Close by energizing the students for participation, feedback, and willingness to understand resets.

VOLCANO RESET POSTERS PREPARATION —

Have whiteboard and whiteboard marker, blank white poster paper, and colored markers, pencils and/or crayons on hand. You may have time to begin posters during this group session or may need to wait until the next group time - depending on how quickly you move through the material. For young students, this can be done as a class to create a Reset Before You Erupt poster to which all participants contribute, rather than each student making their own.

Remember, throughout, to include a "pass" option during circle sharing. Give no energy when students choose to pass. Give frequent recognitions for participating and following the guidelines.

* Ask students: "What is one thing that gets you really upset, annoyed or frustrated while you're riding in the car?" Give each student a chance to respond.
* Then, ask: "What gets you upset, frustrated, angry or sad when you're at home?" and give each student a chance to respond.
* Next, help students to see that in all of these situations, no matter how strong the emotions are, they ultimately do reset themselves…even if they aren't calling it that. Point out also that sometimes, resetting is really hard.
* Brainstorm a list of strategies students use to reset themselves. Go around the circle as many times as you can in order to create a long list of ways to reset. Include some of the ways adults reset or ways you've seen children reset on the list. For example: deep breaths, take a walk, listen to music, play with my dog, count backwards from 10, and so on. Write this brainstormed list on poster paper or on whiteboard— somewhere you can keep it handy for the actual poster-making activity.
* Brainstorm a list of the ways students can benefit from resetting themselves. For example: happy, calm, joyful, a positive experience, peace, stay out of trouble.
* Let students know that at the next meeting, they will be creating their own poster to demonstrate what they've discussed today. The title of the poster will be "Reset Before You Erupt!"
* If there is time, students may begin their posters.
* Throughout, recognize participation, ideas, honesty, clarity, vulnerability, and other great qualities.

VOLCANO RESET POSTERS[5]

For this art activity, have on hand blank white poster paper for each student and colored markers, colored pencils and/or crayons.

Photographs of completed posters are provided on page 92; these are not provided for the group to look at, but to give you, the leader, a few ideas about how they can look. If students seem truly confused about how to complete the posters, you can show them the pictures—just encourage them to create a version that's truly their own.

Poster projects typically will take the entire 30 minutes. If youth have already begun their posters, have them pick up where they left off.

* Give directions (write on whiteboard) for the Reset before You Erupt Posters. Tell students that each poster will need the following:

  ☆ Child's name on front or back
  ☆ Title: Reset Before You Erupt
  ☆ A volcano drawing
  ☆ Lava coming from the top of the volcano (some add fire and lava rocks)
  ☆ On the side of the volcano, list ways to reset
  ☆ Above or around the top of the volcano, between streams of lava, write what you get out of resetting
  ☆ If time allows, add elements like sunshine, rainbows, clouds, thunder clouds, lightning, or rain

* Pass out poster paper along with colorful markers, pencils, and/or crayons.
* When finished, and if you have space in your group meeting place, put the posters up in the shape of a mountain. Create a placard with the title "Reset Before You Erupt" to post at the top.

 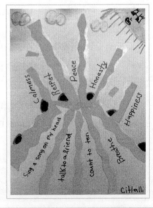

[5] Many thanks to Becky Hauge from Moundsview School in Minnesota for the original idea for these volcano posters.

While completing the "Reset Before You Erupt" poster activity with a group of alternative education high school students, I noticed that one student appeared to not be interested in completing his poster. When running group activities, I never force students to participate fully, and offer recognitions for anything (no matter how small) they're willing to do in the group. I have gone as far as simply recognizing students for showing up to school that day, choosing to come into the group, or for being on time.

This student was struggling to even begin to write reset strategies or what he gets out of resetting on his poster. As I cruised the room and made positive comments about the work going into the posters, I continued to use the idea of "baby steps" to encourage him, and to carefully watch whether he was handling my recognitions well.

Near the end of group time, I noticed that he was writing on and decorating his poster. I walked over and thanked him for completing the project and shared that I loved the way he chose to be honest and transparent in his work. He accepted my recognition and thanked me.

I will never forget what he listed as his reset strategies: sleep and food. What he perceived as the benefits to himself of resetting? Happiness and calm.

His poster was a powerful demonstration of the ways in which many students' most basic needs are not being met. His beautiful willingness to think past what he saw his peers writing and to share his own truth showed that even though he did have real struggles in his life, he could count honesty and openness to being seen as real strengths.

— CE

EGG DROP

Gather materials: whiteboard and whiteboard marker; one raw egg for each small group; and a large shoebox filled with items like cotton balls, paper clips, 4" x 4" squares of aluminum foil, envelopes, rubber bands, a few rolls of tape, sandwich bags, a roll of masking tape, straws, pencils, golf tees, empty cardboard toilet paper or paper towel rolls, pieces of string or yarn, empty lightbulb boxes, Post-It notes, napkins, single paper towels, magnets, push-pins, ribbon, and blank pieces of paper.

* Have participants form partnerships or small groups of no more than three or four.
* Explain that each group will take turns choosing three items at a time from the shoebox; be sure to keep the raw egg carton hidden until all groups have chosen their materials so that participants don't know what the items will be used for until later in the activity. Give each group multiple turns to choose items.
* Once groups have chosen a sufficient number of items, check to see that each group has chosen at least one item that could potentially protect an egg. Distribute additional materials to groups as needed to make sure each has a fair shot at creating a good cushion for the egg drop.
* Explain the challenge: to build protection around a raw egg that will be dropped by one person selected within each group.
* Explain that the person dropping the protected egg will stand on a chair or whatever other elevated surface is available/safe; hold their arm straight up, over their head, in the air; and release the egg.
* Be attentive to any early conversations within the groups about how to choose the best person to drop the egg and keep this in mind for recognitions.
* Provide students with 15 minutes for creation of their egg protector. Students must use only the items their group has chosen.
* As students work, list positive qualities demonstrated by group members during construction on the whiteboard.
* All group members observe as one member from each group drops the egg from the designated area. Restate the expectation that the egg container must be dropped with arm held straight up overhead. Another group member will have the job of opening the egg container to see if the egg survived without cracking.
* Gather students and brainstorm positive qualities they recognized in each other during the project. Add these to the list already started on the whiteboard during the Qualities of Greatness activity. This list could be written on a large piece of poster paper to keep posted in the classroom/group setting.
* To close, have someone read the entire list to the group as a group recognition.

WHAT DO YOU SEE? —

Gather the five images in pages 97 and 98 (three optical illusions, two photos of boys, photo of a teen) and cue up the *Awareness Test* video: https://www.youtube.com/watch?v=oSQJP40PcGI

* Let participants know that you will be showing a few different drawings, and that you would like to have them call out the first thing they see when the drawing is shown.
* Show the three optical illusion drawings (vase/faces, forest/tigers, old lady/young woman), one at a time. Acknowledge whatever students say they see first. Explain that some people may only see one thing when they look at these pictures, and others may see two images that flip back and forth in their perception.
* Have a participant who sees both images point out different features, listing them aloud. For example, you may say, "Point to the old lady's mouth. Point to the young woman's chin." Be sure that all students are able to see both perspectives of each drawing. After each drawing is presented, mention that although everyone is being shown the same drawing, we all see things differently.
* Let students know that you will be showing a photograph (two young boys) and you'd like for them to think about what could be happening in the photo. Call on a few students to share what they think could be going on in the photo. Acknowledge each suggestion.
* Show the photograph of the teenage boy. Ask students to share ideas about what he could be thinking about and why.
* Lead a discussion about how often, we see the same things that others see and yet we have different interpretations. Introduce the idea that we can *choose* how we see things.
* Invite students to think about times when a problem occurred because they saw something differently than someone else. Have they witnessed an adult misunderstanding something that has happened? Misunderstandings can be frustrating. Wouldn't it be helpful if we could all remember that we see things differently?
* Share the Toll Taker story from pages 45-46 of this book.
* Show the Awareness Test video clip. Be willing to show the clip once again if time allows and someone is still struggling to see the dancing bear. If needed, you may have a student actually point out the bear.

* Close with the idea that every day, we all choose our attitudes and how we react to things in our lives. It's great to be able to remember that we all see things differently. Give recognition for participation.

As I taught in a very large 4th grade class—one that included four students who tended to act as ringleaders of disruption—I got to do work with one of my favorite NHA strategies: using the energy of so-called ringleaders to support them in using their intensity in great ways.

These students had been dealt with by other teachers primarily through trips to the office, phone calls home, kind lectures, recess time-outs, and other strategies of the same sort, all without any lasting benefit. I chose the "What Do You See?" activity because I wanted maximum opportunity for students to respond—which some might consider a less than intelligent move in a classroom characterized by disruptive behavior.

What I saw was that this activity would give me the gift of being able to frequently demonstrate giving off-topic or out-of-turn comments zero energy; to give lots of resets and recognitions around resets successfully completed; to recognize often where rules were being followed; and, of course, to unleash positive recognitions to every student who shared appropriately.

By mid-lesson, the ringleaders realized that they were going to get zero attention, relationship or energy from me when they were not behaving. They began to raise their hands and to wait to be called on to share. They appeared to become more focused and engaged in the lesson. Best of all, they appeared to feel good about their new way of participating. I enjoyed every moment; witnessing their transformation was truly a gift.

The teacher filmed the entire lesson and was glad that she did. She shared later on that when feeling frustrated, she could watch small bits of the video clip on her cell phone. This it would help her to reset herself and to continue supporting her students in using their intensity well.

— CE

To find these optical illusions on the Internet: search for "Rubin's Vase"; "tiger optical illusion"; and "Young Girl—Old Woman." Any photos of a single person and a group of people engaged in neutral or positive behaviors will work for the other part of this activity.

QUALITIES OF GREATNESS—EXTREME SPORT

Cue up any video clip of skateboarding, surfing, skiing, skydiving, or other extreme sports, and keep whiteboard and marker on hand for creating lists (see sample below of lists created after watching a skateboarding video).

* Share with your group that you will be showing a video clip of an extreme sport, then show the clip.
* Make 3 columns on the whiteboard: first column, name of sport being watched—we'll use the example of skateboarding here; second column, Filming; third column, Editing. (For younger students, you may want to simplify the activity by only using two columns.)
* Begin with the first column. Ask students to call out what it takes to skate. You may need to begin with a prompting word like "bravery."
* If students call out the name of an object rather than a descriptor—like, "a skateboard"—lead them to positive qualities needed to get your own skateboard: for example, "commitment," if they needed to save money for a board. Make a list with as many positive qualities as the group can name—words like balance, fearlessness, focus, and so on.
* Do the same with the next two columns by asking what positive

qualities it takes to record/film a person who is skateboarding, and then to edit the video. The lists from the first two columns may be similar, and that's fine. When completing the third list, students may suggest words including patience, knowledge, tech-savvy, or smart.

* Lead a discussion about how interesting it is that we are able to name and pinpoint so many positive qualities for each column. What is it that you had to do to list so many qualities? Talk about the thinking the group did to come up with these lists.
* Close with recognition for participation and introduce the thought that if we can develop the skills to see positive qualities in others, we can do the same to see positive qualities in ourselves.

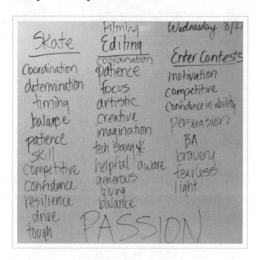

GREATNESS POSTERS

This activity should be taught after students have become very familiar with being able to recognize and list positive qualities. Bring it back repeatedly, or as part of other lessons, until all members of the group have their own poster. You'll need whiteboard, marker, poster paper, and colored markers.

* Tell the group that you will be calling a name to be the first to have their own Greatness Poster created by their classmates.
* Explain that you will randomly choose someone, and that then, everyone else will call out every positive quality they can think of about that person. You will create a list on the board as the qualities are called

out. Mention that over time, this process will be repeated for every person in the group.

* Randomly choose a student and begin creating the list. (See example photographs below.) Support students in *not* listing superficial qualities about their classmates' appearances (nice hair, cool clothes)—unless there is an element of energizing that person's commitment to caring for their appearance or being creative with their fashion or grooming choices.

* The first person chosen to have their positive qualities shared may show some hesitation. Give plenty of recognition for the bravery of being first.

* As group leader, be the first to list a quality for each new group member. Continue to participate in the exercise every time, in case group members have more trouble coming up with qualities for some classmates. This way, if the leader needs to support the group in creating a list for a participant, it's not something that is specific to them.

* As soon as each list is complete, ask for a volunteer to come up and to read the list *to* their peer. Have both students stand up by the whiteboard, facing each other. Encourage the reading volunteer to read the list to their peer instead of reading it about their peer: not "Nick is loyal, kind, funny and generous," but "Nick, you are loyal, kind, funny and generous."

* Make as many individual lists as possible, depending on time.

* Recognize students for being brave enough to watch their peers name their positive qualities, and for participation, honesty, and other qualities of greatness you observe.

* Let everyone have a turn as time allows, and return to this activity each time you are together until all students have their own poster.

* If possible, hang the posters in your classroom or meeting room.

I was leading a challenging group of teenagers through the Greatness Poster activity for the first time. After we finished brainstorming, writing, and creating a poster listing positive qualities of a student, I was amazed that even these students that were difficult to lead enjoyed this activity so much that they actually begged to be the next person for the activity. They loved hearing their peers name their qualities of greatness.

We continued with this activity during every next session, until every single student had a Greatness Poster on the wall. From my vantage point, the most powerful part of the activity was when a student volunteer read the list to their peer face to face. The readers were always sincere, used humor appropriately, and remembered to begin with the language, "You are..."

Hearing qualities of greatness from peers opened doors for inner wealth to begin to be built. This activity lead to students used to shutting out adults to being able to accept the truth about positive recognitions.

— CE

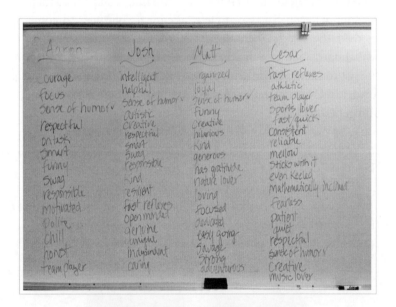

While teaching an alternative education middle school class, I had the great fortune of having an author as a guest speaker. He was one of the most kind, thoughtful, caring and humble men I've ever met. Following his incredibly inspiring presentation, I asked the students to name his qualities of greatness. The guest stood in front of the classroom as the students brainstormed his qualities of greatness; I created a list on the board. When we had a good-sized list, I told him that I wanted to read the list to him.

"I am going to read this list of your qualities of greatness to you and I need you to stand and face me," I said to him. He stood and was fiddling a bit with his presentation items. We stood only a few feet apart. As I began to read the list to him – "You are kind, you are resilient, you are brave" – the energy of receiving positive recognition seemed to hit him all at once. He actually took a small step back and as he listened and took in his qualities of greatness, his eyes filled with tears.

This man had led an extraordinary life: he was a school administrator and a recipient of the prestigious Presidential Fulbright Scholar award. He had taught at an African university, served as a consultant with the government of Nigeria, worked as a department head at UCLA, and been named head of the Peace Corps Training Center in the Caribbean. On that day in our classroom, I was able to witness a tremendously successful man transform as he deeply listened to the qualities of greatness our class had seen in him. It is a moment that I will always treasure, and a memory that reminds me that no one is too old—or too *anything*—to be held and acknowledged in their own greatness.

— CE

INNER WEALTH

Cue up videos: *Greatest Hitter in the World* (http://www.values.com/inspirational-stories-tv-spots/99-the-greatest), *Find Your Greatness Nike Commercial* (https://www.youtube.com/watch?v=2JnYcuRW_qo), and *Jessica Daily Affirmation* (https://www.youtube.com/watch?v=qR3rK0kZFkg)

* Show the *Greatest Hitter in the World* video clip. Ask participants to name the positive qualities in the clip. Lead them to a discussion related to noticing how the boy changed his attitude about what he was doing. Include the idea that the boy was able to reset his thinking to a more positive view. Ask students to identify the moment when this shift in thinking happened in the clip.
* Show the *Find Your Greatness Nike Commercial* video clip. When finished, ask participants to name the positive qualities seen in the runner. Ask them to name what the runner could be doing that he is not doing; then ask, "And what does that say about him?"
* Lead a discussion about the ability to see greatness in even the toughest moments. Share that sometimes it's not easy and takes practice. Let the students know that the more we practice identifying positive qualities, the easier it becomes, even in the most challenging moments. Point out that as we choose to make the best of things and to change our attitude to a more positive one, our Inner Wealth increases. Remind them that Inner Wealth is what we believe to be true about ourselves.
* Share that the last video for this lesson is a demonstration of a very young girl having high levels of Inner Wealth. Show the *Jessica Daily Affirmation* video. This video is a reflection of developmentally appropriate Inner Wealth at the preschool level. When finished, share that just because someone has high levels of Inner Wealth it doesn't mean that they will be seen as boastful or a show-off. Explain that it simply means they see their own positive qualities and can choose to act them out.
* Recognize students for participation and other positive qualities.

RESETTING TO FIND YOUR GREATNESS ⁓

Gather index cards, colored pencils or fine tip colored markers, and crayons; cue up Nike *Find Your Greatness London Olympics Commercial* (https://www. youtube.com/watch?v=WYP9AGtLvRg). When teaching this lesson to very young children, a drawing on the card could be used in place of words.
* Begin the lesson by reminding students that the idea of resetting ourselves may be used in many different ways. We can choose to reset our minds by changing our thoughts; to reset our mouths by choosing not to say something negative; or to reset our actions by not using forms

of physical aggression.

* Invite students to participate in a discussion about any situations when they have chosen to reset themselves. Share a reset story of your own. Make the point that this is for real life, not just for those working to accomplish things at a very high level.
* Show the Nike *Find Your Greatness London Olympics Commercial.*
* Ask for comments related to the commercial or for individual summaries of the video. Ask for insights and connections students have made to their own lives. Share one of your own.
* Pass out index cards to students and encourage them to write their own phrase (mantra) that will help them to reset themselves in their own lives. Have colored pencils, crayons or markers available for color and decoration.
* Provide the opportunity for students to share their cards with the group.
* Give recognition for focus, insight, sharing, bravery, understanding, participation, and other positive qualities.

GUESS MY GREATNESS ACTIVITY

Ahead of the lesson, write single qualities of greatness on 3 x 3 square Post-It notes.

* Have students sit in small groups of 4-5.
* Let them know that they will take turns having a Post-It note on their forehead that has a quality of greatness written on it. Distribute sticky notes to each participant, ensuring that they don't look at the word written on the note before it is their turn to guess.
* Once the student whose turn has come has placed their sticky note on their forehead, each member of the group takes turns describing the ways in which that person might exemplify that specific positive quality in their life. For example: if the Post-It says "helpful," students in the circle could give clues like, "You fix breakfast for your sister every morning." The point is for the person with the Post-It on their forehead to guess which positive quality is written on their note.
* After the first student guesses their own positive quality, the person on their right will place their Post-It on their forehead, and the activity will continue until everyone has had a turn.

* Provide support as needed to help define words being used or to give help for clues when needed.
* Energize students for following the rules, not peeking at their words, and coming up with clear clues, as well as for participation.
* Variations on this activity: writing the names of professions on the Post-It notes and asking students to list qualities of greatness needed for each job, or writing the names of successful, well-known people on the Post-Its and having students name their positive qualities while other students try to guess the name on their note.

GREATNESS TRUTH CIRCLE

This activity supports youth in owning their qualities of greatness and in recognizing their commonalities and differences.

* Have the entire group form a large circle, all facing into the center.
* Invite students to take one step into the middle of the circle if the statements you read out are true for them. Share an example like, "I have a great sense of humor," or "I have been to Mexico," and demonstrate the step-in as though it is true for you; make clear that if it is not true for them, they should remain standing without stepping in. Also demonstrate how to look around the group and see who else has stepped in, and then how to step back to get ready for the next statement.
* Make a thorough list of statements before starting the activity. Tailor it to your group, providing statements that encourage identification and ownership of qualities of greatness, intermingled with statements reflecting details of students' lives to help them notice their commonalities and differences.

Example statements:
I own a dog.
I have at least one brother.
I am helpful.
I am artistic.
I have someone that I miss a lot.
I love music.
I am compassionate.

I want to travel the world.
I don't know my father.
I am funny.

* Be clear that this is a silent activity. Reset students if they talk while it is in process. Regularly give recognitions to those following the guidelines. Include recognition for willingness to step into the center alone or with only a few classmates.
* Continue the activity until you have only a couple of minutes left. If there is time, you can have students in the circle come up with statements themselves. This can be tricky with older students; they may offer up statements that are inappropriate for school. If this happens, simply reset them and move on.
* Finish the day with recognitions of students for their participation, respectfulness, and any other qualities you have observed.

OWN YOUR QUALITIES OF GREATNESS

A reinforcing activity that builds on the previous one. Have whiteboard and marker handy.

* Share the truth that we all have good days and bad days. Encourage students to think about a good or great day they've had in the recent past, or even a challenging day with some good in the middle of it.
* Invite students to share a situation where they did something or behaved in a way that helped their day or someone else's day be better. Ask them to share the story in the clearest way possible. Students may take turns in a circle or share after raising their hands, popcorn-style.
* As students speak, recognize them for their honesty and willingness to share. Provide each storyteller with the greatest possible level of your focus. As soon as each story is shared, list on the whiteboard qualities of greatness that you noticed during their story. By the time all students have shared, you should have a good-sized list on the board.
* Following the storytelling and creation of the list of qualities of greatness, invite students to take a close look at the list and to find three qualities that they believe they possess.
* Next, have each student in the group say the items they've chosen for

themselves in the following way: "I am helpful, kind and funny."

* Recognize the group once again for participation, honesty, thoughtfulness, and other great qualities.
* Depending on the age of the group members and their reading ability, you may choose to adjust the qualities of greatness listed on the board. For some groups, you might choose to use visuals (pictures) in place of written words, or to use both a word and a visual for each quality.

ONE-ON-ONE ENERGIZING

This activity helps students to feel comfortable with seeing qualities of greatness in others; to become comfortable with sharing what they see with peers; and to accept the qualities others see in them.

I have seen this activity successfully done with all age groups. Younger children may need extra coaching. When doing this for the first time, students may share more superficial aspects of the qualities—for example, "You have nice hair." Encourage them to go more deeply, and to use words that describe their classmate's active role in creating the thing they are acknowledging: "You take good care of your appearance and yourself."

* Share with students that you are impressed with their ability to understand the words we use to describe qualities of greatness. Let them know that you have seen them accept the recognitions you've given to them since the start of the group.
* Explain that the group will participate in an activity where two volunteers will stand up facing each other and will have 30 seconds each to energize their partner.
* Getting the first pair to participate may be challenging. One idea that has worked well is to ask if anyone would like to do One-on-One Energizing with you. If there are two adults in the group or classroom, the two adults could model the activity.
* As students recognize each other, listen and keep time. As soon as the first student finishes, have the second student begin their 30 seconds immediately.
* When each pair finishes, ask each person how it felt to name the positive qualities of their peer, and also how it felt to hear another student point out their positive qualities. Energize them for their bravery, honesty,

vulnerability, and willingness to share their thoughts.

* Complete as many sessions as possible in the group time. This is a wonderful activity to complete any time there is extra time during your groups.

NAME YOUR GREATNESS OF THE DAY [6]

This activity supports youth in recognizing that even when they have a challenging day, there is always something to appreciate in themselves or others. Have on hand note paper and pen or whiteboard and marker—whatever is needed to record student shares, which you will later use to make small posters for your classroom featuring those shares.

* Ask students to think about something that was great about their current day. If group is held early in the morning, have them think of something from the previous day.
* Encourage students to share what they believe is something great about their day. Use the idea of Baby Steps to remind them that sometimes, finding gratitude even for the tiniest things is valuable and can help us to reset ourselves. When everyone has completed the task of naming something that has gone well, begin the process of having them share, out loud to the group, the positive qualities that go along with each comment. For example: "I am responsible." "I take care of myself." "I am well behaved." Be sure to energize them along the way as they share even the smallest successes. If students struggle to think of something great to share, and they can only name things that would not be considered great, coach them to re-frame them in greatness.
* The group leader records these statements on the whiteboard or paper as they are shared, then—outside of group time—makes a small poster for each that can be hung in the space where group meetings are held. Distill them as needed to make them brief and clear: "I made it to school on time." "I remembered to bring my lunch." "I stayed out of trouble all day long."
* Post the comments in the group meeting room or classroom if possible. If not, put them up for the next group meeting.

[6] Thanks to Chris Berry, a teacher from Rocklin, California, for creating this activity.

* Recognize students for their willingness to have their comments posted and any other qualities you notice. Further reveal to them what these statements say about them. For example, it takes ongoing restraint and thoughtfulness, as well as mindful kindness and decision-making "to stay out of trouble all day long."

GREATNESS CIRCLE ━

This activity supports students in knowing that positive qualities can always be found and pointed out to others.

* Invite students to form a circle in the meeting room or classroom. Students may stand or sit.
* Ask group members to take turns thanking their peers for something they appreciate, or for something that peer did for them or another classmate.

* This activity works best when students share in order around the circle. Where any student chooses to pass, give that choice little energy. Recognize that person for participation and quickly move on to the next student.
* As leader/teacher, give a recognition for every comment. Point out qualities like being insightful, aware, and open minded.
* Continue until the end of class time. If students get off track with their positive comments and recognitions, reset them to positive comments only.
* Recognize the group for participation, telling the truth, and being brave enough to speak up in front of the group.

During a semester of coaching a kindergarten teacher who was struggling to manage the intensity of a large and energetic class, I suggested she try having her entire class sit in a circle following her morning "sitting on the carpet as a whole class" routine. She immediately shared concerns to them being able to sit respectfully in a circle long enough to pay attention and participate. I heard her concerns and encouraged her to give it a try and that I would be there to help her if needed.

I supported her in stating clear rules for the Greatness Circle time. They were something like: no standing, no touching other students, and no calling out when it's not your turn. She asked her students to acknowledge hearing the rules by giving a thumbs up or a thumbs down if they weren't sure they understood. I was able to model recognizing students along the way, and the teacher recognized students for paying attention and following her directions. It was wonderful to witness more students participating as they saw their teacher recognizing students for their participation.

This teacher went on reviewing the rules until everyone understood. She then shared that the students would take turns, one at a time, saying something they appreciated about the friend to their left, assuring them that it would be okay to share a tiny thing like, "I'm glad you're sitting next to me nicely." She also made it clear that it was okay to say "pass" this first time around if they had nothing to say when it was their turn. She began by modeling a simple appreciation to the student on her left, then guided that student to appreciate the next student in the circle.

It was miraculous to watch this group of intense kindergartners acknowledging each other. The teacher practiced recognizing each student for their contribution; supported those struggling in the moment; and thanked those taking a pass for following the guidelines. At the end of the circle sharing, she asked if those who'd passed would like another turn, and a few of them took the opportunity.

If you can imagine having 25 or more energetic five-year-olds sitting in circle together and completing this activity in a responsible way, you can imagine how it felt for this teacher. It gave her hope. She gained more trust in her students and was able to continue the day with a refreshingly positive atmosphere that I'm sure was felt by everyone in the room.

— CE

Chapter Seven

MORE GKI ACTIVITIES

These activities are useful as add-ons for the sequence described in Chapter Six. Once you have a feel for those activities, you may decide to substitute these for others listed in that chapter.

While the activities in Chapter Six were designed and have been implemented mostly for classroom use, all of the activities in this chapter are meant to be useful across a variety of settings: in classrooms, at home, or in other kinds of groups (foster care, treatment programs).

THE HUMAN RATING SCALE ACTIVITY

This activity gives students/children a chance to reflect on where they radiate the most energy, relationship, time, and attention in their day-to-day lives.

* Begin with an introduction of the purpose of this activity: to be honest with ourselves about where we give out energy, relationship, time and attention in our daily lives, and to have an active, conscious experience of considering and measuring this for ourselves.
* Explain to the group that the right side of the room represents the number 10 and the far left side of the space represents the number

zero, similar to a number line.

* If the group has 10 or fewer people in it, have the whole group proceed to the next step; if there are more than 10, start with a subgroup of participants (6-8).

* Have participants stand in the middle of the room, where the imaginary 5 would be.

* Facing the participants, explain that you, as the leader, will be saying some words and phrases. They will need to move to the area on the rating scale that matches the level of energy, relationship, or emotion they sense with each statement: a zero would mean that they typically give no energy or participation to the action/situation, while a 10 would mean that they tend to give that action/situation a lot of energy or participation.

* Clarify that they can base their response simply on their internal reactions (not acted out) or on whether they are likely to get involved when these things come up in their lives. For example: when bullying is mentioned, some could choose to stand at a 10 because it's very upsetting to them, or because they often become involved in bullying—whether as a perpetrator, victim, or bystander/ally.

* Advise the group that honesty will support them getting the most from this activity, and that if judgement about self or others comes up, a self-reset would be appropriate. Make sure everyone understands; answer any questions before proceeding.

* Read out the listed situations; add or subtract as needed, adding any situations not listed that would serve your group. The more situations mentioned, the better:

A lack of patience shown by adults
Arguments in the car
Being interrupted
Being teased
Being told "no"
Being told what to do
Cell phone use in public
Cheating on school work
Chores
Continuous pencil tapping
Dishonesty (being lied to by friends)

Dishonesty (being lied to by parents/caregivers)
Disorganization
Dress code violations
Eye rolling by adults
Inappropriate noises
Inappropriate outbursts by others during meals, classroom time
Lack of communication by peers/adults
Lack of preparation
Lectures given by adults
Long car rides
Observation of bullying
Others being tardy
Peers throwing things
Profanity
Rules at home
Rules at school
Yelling

* As each statement is read out, support participants to move to the place on the rating scale that reflects their real-life reactions/responses. Give reminders when needed. Give participants time between situations to deeply consider where they want to stand.
* When finished with the list, recognize participants for the participation, thoughtfulness, honesty, and courage expressed through their responses (Stand Two), and ask them to be seated.

We all react differently to similar situations. Our reactions to the same set of circumstances can shift a lot, depending on mood or other personal factors. Guide students to consider noticing when they are giving their energy to something that isn't good for themselves or others; and to then consider practicing the self-reset in a way that allows them to deal with the situation at hand—without giving it energy (Stand One). Remind them that giving their energy in response to drama, conflict, or other negative situations or interactions like the ones in the Human Rating Scale activity is most likely to create worse problems.

Discuss the ways in which reacting more appropriately could improve the outcome: by not escalating situations, by keeping the young person out of trouble, by maintaining the young person's inner peace, and so on.

STAND ONE ROLE PLAYING —

To prepare for the activity, pass out index cards to every member of the group. Ask group members to write down annoying actions or behaviors that bother them in real life. Put all the cards in a hat/box for a drawing.

* Review Stand One. Hold a discussion about what it really means to refuse to energize negativity. Does it mean ignoring? Does it mean not speaking to the person that's bothering us?
* If age-appropriate, lead the discussion into brainstorming ways we give attention to negativity without realizing—ways we reveal that we have an emotional reaction or charge in response to negativity. Examples might be eye-rolling or using a certain tone of voice.
* Have a group member choose a card from the hat. Ask them to act out the behavior on the card, and then have another group member practice (1) giving the behavior no energy and then (2) asking them to stop the behavior without giving it energy.
* Midway through participants having their turns acting out negative behaviors and practicing giving no energy, attention, or relationship, introduce the idea of them giving simple recognitions to their partner after the unwanted behavior stops—reinforcing Stand Two: nurturing and creating success.
* Continue with the same process until everyone in the group has a turn both acting out a behavior and practicing using Stand One. With a very small group (less than five), you may want to include yourself as a participant.
* During this activity, there will be many opportunities to model giving recognitions to participants for staying on task, following the activity guidelines, acting out the behavior in a clear way, and authentically refusing to energize the behaviors in an authentic way.

After completion, lead a discussion of the activity, providing frequent group recognitions. Discuss that this may have seemed easy in a structured activity like this one—but that in real life, when challenging emotions (anger, frustration, annoyance, sadness) are running high, sticking with Stand One may be challenging. Remind participants that getting good at Stand One takes practice and patience. Point out that most people may need to reset themselves in order to not give energy to a behavior. This is a wonderful example of weaving together the Three Stands.

During an NHA mentoring phone call with an amazing mother of five, we explored some particular challenges with Stand One: namely, the difficulties involved in teaching siblings not to give energy, relationship or attention to a brother or sister who is displaying negative behaviors. We talked about how typically, when one child is off track, siblings or peers respond with the same level of negativity; and before we know it, the entire family or class is off track.

We discussed skills to use in those moments: recognizing those who are choosing to give no attention to negativity and giving resets along the way, as well as using Creative Recognitions. We talked about how important it is to be able to reset ourselves when faced with these moments (or hours) of high-level challenges. We also discussed the importance of increasing use of Stand Two and providing recognitions when things are going well. As we got deeper into our discussion we did some role-plays, practicing using the negativity we were feeling as fuel for positivity. We practiced by choosing to be grateful for our honest discussion and for being able to discuss these issues openly, and for being on a path of problem-solving instead of hopelessness.

My mentee, who happens to be an experienced and talented trainer in NHA and who uses NHA in her career as a social worker, tried the role-play described above. She reported that her children— ranging from elementary age to high school age—participated and were fully engaged. They enjoyed plenty of laughter while acting out misbehaviors and practicing clear limits with each other.

An example of one of the behaviors pulled from the hat was about talking too loud while being in another person's space. When those behaviors were acted out, the sibling practicing Stand One responded by giving minimal energy and calmly saying (à la Stand Three), "I need you to give me space," or "Please take two steps back." When the acting-out didn't immediately stop, that sibling practiced turning away instead of responding to the negative behaviors.

As each child finished their role playing and practice, Mom was able to give heartfelt and honest recognitions for high-level participation. One of the biggest takeaways from the experience was that siblings realized they only have control over themselves. How about that for a great life lesson?

For fun, the family came up with an extension to this activity: siblings and parents gave each other points every time they were seen or experienced refusing to energize negativity. No one recorded or kept track of points, except for maybe the youngest in the family. The mother shared with me that she gave herself points when she caught herself being able to reset and refusing to energize negativity: all great reminders to keep up use of Stand One.

— CE

WHERE IS MY LINE? —

Children typically learn right from wrong through experimenting with boundaries. This starts early, and this experimentation brings them to a personal sense of and investment in doing the right thing. Establishment of clear boundaries and rules for themselves sets the stage for their ability to notice themselves being off-track and resetting. These activities support youth in learning to use the reset as their primary strategy for being their best version of themselves.

* Open up a discussion with your family, students or youth group participants related to the idea that we all have internal guidance about what we will or will not do in our lives. Include the notion that although we have this guidance, it takes a certain level of awareness to notice when we are feeling off-track or on track with our choices. Words and phrases like *intuition, inner-self, instinct, inner voice* and *gut feelings* are important to include as a way to develop the idea of raising levels of self-awareness. Discuss that sometimes in life, things happen so quickly that it can be challenging to make quick decisions, especially when we feel like we're "on the spot" and under pressure to make a decision. This is true for people of all ages.
* Create a line with painters' tape or masking tape on the floor. If you are unable to use tape on the floor, create an imaginary line or place a thin rope or string across the floor. If the group is outside, you can use

sidewalk chalk. Be sure that the line is long enough for all participants to have space to stand on either side of the line during the activity.

* Designate one side of the line as YES and the other side of the line as NO.
* Have everyone stand in a neutral area away from the line to begin.
* Tell participants that you will say a phrase or describe a situation, and that each of them will have the opportunity to decide if they would do the thing mentioned or not. When their decision is made, they will move to the yes or no side of the line. If they are unsure, they may choose to stand on the line.
* Ask everyone to remain quiet while deciding on yes or no. Tell them that a discussion can be had following everyone making their choice about where to stand.
* As participants make their choices, be sure to recognize participation, giving thought to situations, and sharing comments about decisions made. Use language related to being aware while making decisions, being thoughtful in decision-making, and realizing that we make our own choices. These recognitions can be part of the discussion held with the group or individual in between situations being read.

Phrases and situations will vary greatly depending on the age group participating in the activity. For younger children, they might read:

☆ There is a cookie on the counter and it's not time for a snack. Will you eat it before snack time?
☆ There is a long line at the drinking fountain. Will you wait in line instead of trying to take cuts?
☆ Your mom said you can watch a video about baby animals. She leaves the room. Do you switch over to a playing a video game?
☆ Kids are running on the playground. You see someone fall down. Do you stop to see if they're okay?

While writing up this activity, I asked my four-year-old grandson if he would help me out by trying it. He agreed quickly, very curious about what I was going to ask him to do. We went through the activity, using a yardstick to show the boundary between "yes" and "no." After I read each statement and question, he paused and thought about the choice he would make, then moved with excitement to one side of the ruler. I was happy to see that he made the appropriate choices, and yet was most pleased to see that he took the time to think about it. After we finished our experiment, I recognized him for helping me and talked with him about how he gets to make his own choices. He was very proud of himself and gave me a big hug.

— CE

For older children:

☆ You are doing homework on your home computer. When you parents leave the computer area, do you minimize the homework and start playing a video game?

☆ You are in a store with a friend and they tell you that they're really good at stealing packs of gum. When they suggest that you give it a try, do you decide to try it out for yourself?

☆ You're on the playground with your friends waiting in line for a turn at swinging. You hear one of your friends saying to another friend, "Your shirt is stupid." You can see that your friend may have hurt feelings by the look on her face. Do you say something to help make her feel better?

☆ Your parents have a rule about no snacks before dinner. Dinner time is in 30 minutes, yet you see freshly baked cookies on the kitchen counter. Do you eat one?

For teenagers:

☆ You are scheduled to have a math test after lunch time at school. When you arrive at school, you see a classmate passing out copies of the test answer key to a small group of friends. She offers one to you.

Do you accept it?

☆ It's a minimum day at school. You're walking home with a group of friends. One of them invites everyone over to hang out because their parents won't be home until after work. Your parents do not allow you to spend time at friends' homes without parents being there. Do you go to the friend's house anyway?

☆ You are spending the night at your friend's house. Her older brother has his driver's license and invites you and his sister to go along for a midnight ride. Do you go along for the ride?

Feel free to write up your own scenarios based on age groups and situations you'd like to offer practice for with your children, students, or youth group members.

MAKING MY OWN CLEAR RULES

This activity guides participants in creating rules for themselves.

☆ Lead a discussion about the fact that we all have rules to follow. We have laws for our society, school rules, and rules in our homes. Sometimes rules are written and even posted; sometimes they are implied.

☆ Acknowledge that sometimes the rules aren't clear. Explain that we can actually create our own set of rules and expectations.

☆ Talk about rule-breaking: in particular, the fact that breaking a rule – their own or someone else's – isn't the end of the world. They can reset and get back on track to follow the rule the next time the opportunity comes up. They can also appreciate themselves for every rule they are able to follow, whenever they do follow it.

☆ Ask the family, class, or group to brainstorm and share out ideas for rules they'd like to have for themselves. Create a list of shared ideas on a poster paper or whiteboard.

☆ Start by giving and writing down a few examples of rules you may have for yourself as an adult. For example, you could begin with:

No hitting my snooze button on my alarm in the morning.
No eating junk food or drinking sugary sodas or coffee drinks at work.
No staying up past 10:00 on work nights.

No spending money on fast food.
No yelling at my children.

☆ Work to encourage all participants to give ideas for their own rules. Recognize them along the way for participation, as well as their willingness to be honest and to share in front of the group.
☆ Once you've created a good-sized recorded list that can be used to inspire rule-making, pass out lined paper for everyone to write up a draft of their own rules. Encourage everyone to come up with at least five rules for themselves. During this part of the process, ask for volunteers willing to share their ideas with the group. Provide participants with individual and group recognitions for wonderful ideas for rules.
☆ Next, pass out poster paper and colorful markers, and encourage participants to list their clear rules in a way that makes sense to them. They may want to decorate their rules with drawings or stickers, or they may choose to simply write them out.
☆ Have participants create a title for their rules; titles can be a simple as "John's Rules" or "My Rules."
☆ Support the group members in ideas for where they would like to hang their posters. Have everyone share ideas and their reasons for where they'd like to place their posters.

Share the idea that some of them may like to write their rules in their phones or in their school binders or notebooks as a way to remember their rules during the day.

In closing, remind the participants that when rules are broken, they can choose to reset and try again the next day; that they can appreciate themselves for rule *following;* and that rules can always be adjusted, removed and changed. If time allows, end also with appreciating the group and individuals for the rules they have not broken. Reveal to them how this reflects great restraint, wisdom, and healthy use of power and control.

FOUR CORNERS: RESETS —

This activity gives groups an opportunity to think about the idea of being reset and/or resetting themselves. It will also give you a chance to see how your group members feel about resets. Encourage self-reflection and honesty.

Let the group know that there will be no judgement and that honesty will make this activity even more powerful.

* Point to one corner in the room and say, "When I say 'go,' move to *this* corner of the room if you know nothing or very little about resets or resetting yourself."
* Point to the next corner and say, "When I say 'go,' move to *this* corner if you are familiar with resets and resetting yourself…and if you don't like being reset or the idea of resetting yourself."
* Pointing to the third corner in the room, say, "When I say 'go,' move to *this* corner if you feel that you have a pretty good understanding of being reset and/or resetting yourself; if you work at it, and if you kind of like the idea of resetting."
* Lastly, point to the fourth corner of the room and say, "When I say 'go,' move to this corner of the room if you have working very hard on accepting resets given to you by others and have been working on ways to reset yourself…if you feel that you're getting good at resets, and can honestly say that you see resets as a gift."
* Provide participants with plenty of thinking time as they move around the room and choose a corner. Often, group members will struggle with which corner they should stand in. Reassure them that it's fine to go with their gut feelings.
* When everyone has chosen a corner, recognize the entire group for making their honest choice and for following instructions.
* Then give your full attention to one group of participants at a time. Provide them with heartfelt recognitions for the corner they chose and what that says about them. These recognitions could sound like this:

Corner 1: "Wow, I really appreciate your honesty. You could have chosen to stand in a different corner so that everyone wouldn't know that you know very little about resets, yet you were brave enough to stand here. Right now, you are demonstrating honesty, integrity and bravery. Thank you for standing in the place that best suits you."

Corner 2: "Look at you, choosing honesty over everything else right now. Your willingness to stand here in front of everyone and let them know that you don't really like resets is you being courageous. Thanks for being honest and choosing to stand in the corner that matches how you feel about being reset and the idea of resetting yourself."

Corner 3: "Thank you, everyone, for choosing this corner. I can see that you were willing to demonstrate that while you have a good understanding of resets, you may not feel totally confident quite yet. I appreciate your honesty and your ability to be so aware of your own understanding. You are so insightful."

Corner 4: "Look at all of you choosing the corner where you are able to own the gift of being reset and the gift of resetting yourselves. You are showing that you are dedicated and open-minded, and that you have an awareness of knowing when you need to reset. Thank you."

* It's also a great idea to notice how many participants are in each corner. You can find a way to recognize the varying sizes of the groups. If there is only one person or a small group in any corner, they can be recognized for not being afraid to stand alone or in a small group when most everyone else chose different corners.
* After recognizing all four corners, ask everyone to return to their seats while giving further whole group recognitions for honesty and integrity.
* Next, hold a discussion to dig deeper into what it feels like to be reset; how it feels to reset others; and strategies that are useful for resetting yourself. Provide guiding questions and recognitions but allow most of the brilliance to emerge here from participants' sharing.
* Remember to recognize participants for not criticizing or giving unsolicited advice about where others should be standing. If the leader of the activity knows group members well, specific recognitions pointing out times when they've observed participants taking resets or resetting themselves can be very useful.
* If the discussion lends itself to strategies used by group members for resetting themselves, a list could be written on a poster sheet or whiteboard as a visual for everyone.

After I completed the Four Corners: Resets activity and led the closing discussion in a 5th grade class, students shared some stunningly wise insights, including:

"Even though I know how to reset myself, sometimes when my teacher resets me I have to reset my own disappointment from being reset by my teacher in the first place."

"I have realized that if I don't reset myself and I don't take a reset from my teacher, then bad plus bad equals worse."

"I know that I should probably reset myself as much as I can, because you only get this day one time."

The level of wisdom that comes from young people learning the basic strategies of NHA for themselves is always incredible to me. After many years of practicing NHA with others and on myself, I can confidently say that children of all ages are naturally able to understand and complete resets better than the adults who show up to teach them about resets.

— CE

RESETS: NEGATIVE THOUGHTS VS. STRONG EMOTIONS

This activity helps students to distinguish between resetting of negative thoughts and strong emotions.

* Discuss Stand One.
* Have the group consider: what causes you upset (anger, annoyance, frustration, impatience….)?
* Pass out Post-It notes, three to each person.
* Ask everyone to write three things that bother them, one on each note. Give hints for a variety of settings: at home, in school, in a car with friends…
* Collect the Post-Its.
* As a group, put the Post-It notes into groups based on common themes on a whiteboard, wall, or poster board.
* Review each thematic group, then create a sentence representing each theme, beginning with: "I refuse to energize…"
* Have group members take turns reading the sentences created together.
* After each one is read, discuss what it would be like to reset yourself in the heat of the moment when that thing is happening.

A DAY IN REAL LIFE —

This activity will take up two to three sessions—possibly more for very large groups.

* Lead a discussion about how a typical day for most of us includes ups and downs, successes and struggles, good times and hard times. Ask participants to share the basics of what a typical day would look like for them. How do they feel about a typical day most of the time? How do people respond to you on a typical day? At the end of most days, how do they feel: beaten down and not listened to, or hopeful and celebrated?
* At the end of the discussion, introduce the idea that we have the opportunity to choose to focus on the negative or on the positive. Point out a couple of negative things shared in the discussion on which one could choose to focus; then, point out some positives. Compare the impact of focusing on the negative to the impact of focusing on the positive.
* Pass out half-sheets of paper. Ask each group member to write about something that has been an ongoing struggle for them. Examples might be: being late to school most mornings and receiving negative comments from the office staff or teacher, being rushed to get ready in the morning by a parent or being told that they need to try harder.
* Ask each group member to share their struggle out loud and then to crumple their paper. Explain that they can use the energy of how the struggle made them feel to appreciate things that have gone well.
* Next, have participants (best on the same day they've shared and crumpled paper with negative comments) use the energy from the struggles to shift into thinking about and writing something that they appreciate or goes well for them (even the tiniest success) on another ½ sheet of paper.
* Ask each group member to share their success out loud with the group. Give recognitions along the way for participants being willing to move from negativity in their lives to positivity. Encourage them to focus on and notice how the shift makes them feel. Mention that sometimes it takes time to feel and use the negative energy and then to transform it into positive energy.

In closing, discuss how with practice this strategy for choosing to focus on what's going well and using negative energy for positive fuel can change days from being bad or neutral to good and even great.

WALL OF GREATNESS —

This activity is a great way to publicly recognize expressions of greatness.

* Create a bulletin board space with the title "Wall of Greatness." This space is for any demonstrations of success that emerge. This is not only a place for perfect papers; it is a place for demonstrations of effort, perseverance, hard work, or any other positive quality. For example: If a child often fails math tests and receives a 69 percent, that would be something worth posting; or if they often refuse to draw or color, but then decide to try it, that would also be worth posting.
* Post papers and other items collage-style.
* Keep the idea of Baby Steps (recognition for even the smallest successes) in mind!

GREATNESS GRAFFITI —

This activity is another creative way to keep positive recognitions flowing.

* Provide a space for yourself and for students to write positive comments about each other. Large poster-sized notepads or poster flip charts work well for this positive strategy. Hang the writing surface on the wall with the title Greatness Graffiti and a colored marker attached.
* The rules for Greatness Graffiti are:

  ☆ Anyone may write positive comments about anyone else in the class.
  ☆ Only one person writes at a time.
  ☆ If negative comments or pictures appear, the page will simply be removed (without discussion) and a new sheet will be made available for the next positive comment.

It's a great idea for you, the adult in charge, to make regular additions to the Greatness Graffiti wall. Make sure that every child in the household, classroom, or group is commented on.

INTENTIONAL ENERGIZING BY ADULT —

This activity offers an opportunity for you to directly energize individual students in front of others.

* Randomly choose someone to receive positive recognitions from you for a few minutes in front of others. Speak *to* the child, not about them. Insert them into the *'beingness'* of the quality – for example, "Jennifer, I noticed how respectful and kind you are being with your classmates. Those are great qualities I see in you."
* This is a great strategy to begin the day, a class period, or the time immediately following the lunch break. It's also a good one for families to do around the dinner table.
* Only those who are present may be chosen—this can serve as great motivation to show up.

MYSTERY GREATNESS —

This is a wonderful strategy to for beginnings or endings of time together. It is an engaging way to fold the entire group into energizing one participant, guided by the group leader or teacher.

* Secretly choose someone, then begin giving recognitions out loud in front of the class without stating the name of the person who has been chosen.
* Start with broad and general recognitions that could be true for many.
* Become more specific with your recognitions as you name them, with the goal of others in the group being able to solve the mystery by guessing who you are recognizing. Be sure to complete your recognitions even after everyone successfully identifies the recipient.

PEER ENERGIZING —

This activity is a great way to offer a break from hard work.

* Ask for two volunteers to stand in front of the class facing each other.

Each student has 30 seconds to energize (give positive recognitions) to their peer.

* When both students have had a turn to give and to receive recognitions, ask how it felt to give and also to receive.
* Often, when the students are new to this activity, they may point out superficial qualities. Honor all recognitions offered while encouraging more meaningful recognitions.
* Recognize both students for demonstrating honesty, bravery, being fearless, speaking from their hearts, and so on.

DAILY QUALITY OF GREATNESS CHARTS

These charts are a suitable replacement for pulling cards (red, yellow and green each representing a negative, positive or so-so behavior) or any other stoplight or behavior system matching a range of behaviors.

* Create colorful laminated cards naming individual qualities of greatness.
* Hang them where they are clearly visible.
* Write children's names on wooden clothespins.
* When children demonstrate behaviors related to the positive qualities listed on the cards, simply clip the clothespin to the card. Use of clothespins allows for clipping multiple children's names to the same card.

WEB OF GREATNESS

This activity is meant to give educators and families another way to publicly acknowledge students' and family members' qualities of greatness.

* Write one or a few qualities of greatness on a whiteboard at the start of class or family time.
* Write student/family names underneath specific qualities as students/children demonstrate them throughout the time you are together.

OR:

* Create a poster-sized "word web" visual and laminate it. Be sure there

are enough circles for the entire class/family or make one without circles (lines only).

* Write a new quality of greatness in the center each day/period. As students/children demonstrate that specific quality, write their name in a circle or at the end of a line. This is easy to erase at the end of the day or class time.

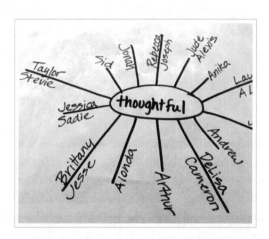

Add to the impact of these activities of naming greatness with a review of the names at the end of the class period or day.

FLASHCARDS: POSITIVE QUALITIES/SITUATIONS

A fun, creative way to amp up capacity for and creativity with Stand Two recognitions.

* Brainstorm qualities of greatness with group by sharing aloud with each other. Children may share qualities such as: helpful, loyal, funny, smart, kind, artistic, responsible, athletic...
* Recognize group for their contributions. Pass out 3-4 small Index cards to each participant and ask them to write a quality of greatness (one per card) so that a stack of qualities of greatness flashcards is created.
* Collect the cards and if the same qualities are listed more than once keep them in the stack of flashcards.
* Shuffle the flashcards and place face down on a table or the floor. Group members will take turns choosing a flashcard, reading the quality of

greatness to the group and then sharing an example of evidence of that quality. For instance, a flashcard may have "loyal" written on it and the participant could share "a friend who sticks by your side no matter what happens."

* Extension: Follow the same procedure above, yet have participants write short descriptions of a variety of situations. Follow the same steps and when children choose situation flashcards, they will be asked to share a quality of greatness that matches the situation listed on the flashcard. For example, a card may include, "A kid organized his homework and backpack." The participant choosing that card and reading aloud may follow with, "This kid is organized" or simply "organized" or "effective planning."

POSITIVE PHONE CALLS

Teachers and group leaders can use these calls to fold parents and caregivers into the NHA/GKI magic. Parents can make calls to others about their child/ren too.

* Make a point of calling parents or caregivers with great and good reports about their child, rather than calling when something has gone wrong with the child.
* Long story short: Do it! I've had parents of challenging children cry when I call with good feedback because they live in fear of the school calling with more bad news; and I've had other parents cry because they rarely hear from the school about their well-behaved student.

A BOY NAMED WALTER

To prepare for this activity, order a copy of the book *A Boy Named Walter* by Les and Genny Nuckolls. This is the true story of a boy who began his life as an orphan living in multiple foster care situations. The book's reading level is grades 4-6; however, this lesson has been used successfully in middle and high school alternative education settings as well.

Read the book aloud together in the classroom, family, or youth group setting. Depending on the age and reading level of participants, the facilitator may read the entire story to the group over multiple sessions or as a segment of sessions including other activities. You may also choose to let group members take turns reading aloud.

Following each chapter, lead a discussion where participants have the opportunity to name the qualities of greatness displayed by Walter, and the evidence the author provides for the named quality of greatness. You can try listing those qualities and the evidence for each quality on a whiteboard or worksheet. Refer to the list of qualities of greatness on pages 53-55 in this book to guide discussions. Also guide students to recognize opportunities to name what Walter could have chosen to do, yet did *not* do.

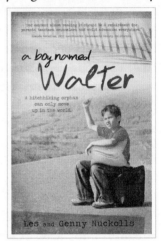

This story is a great tool for leading participants to name what they are grateful for in their own lives, and through the lens of the intention of Baby Steps. Be sure to recognize readers and those sharing qualities and evidence along the way during this activity.

SUPPORTING YOUTH IN RESETTING WITH PARENTS/GUARDIANS

This activity is designed for group leaders or teachers who work with youth who share about difficulties getting along with their parents. An interesting point comes up over and over with all ages of kids: they say that they fight with their parents often, and that things escalate so quickly that they have no idea how the whole thing started.

* Discuss this topic with GKI students in terms of energy and relationship patterns, and how NHA strategies can be used to break those patterns that lead to fighting. It generally comes back to students getting better at resetting themselves when annoyed or frustrated by their parents.
* Brainstorm strategies with youth who have been working with NHA for a while. Here are some strategies that have come up in these discussions with GKI groups; your groups will come up with their own:

    ☆ Reset to let it go. Do not give your energy to negative actions, even in your thoughts. Instead, think, "I'll reset and let it go," and ask yourself whether it is really such a big deal for the parent to have their way (e.g. if they want the child to do something *right now* that the child does not want to do)?

☆ When things are going well, share this with your parents: "We're learning about resetting ourselves at school in our group, and I'm going to practice resetting myself when you and I are struggling." You can simply leave it at that or take the opportunity to explain in your own words what a reset is.

☆ If there are frequent battles around homework, begin to do it as soon as you get home. Tell your parent that you have homework and that you are doing it right away. Let the parent know also that on days you do not have homework, you will let them know that as soon as you get home. If the parent chooses not to believe you, reset; without giving energy, show the parent through whatever means you have that you are telling the truth (show them your online school record where assignments are tracked, show your backpack contents, or whatever other way you have to demonstrate this).

☆ Be sure to thank your parent when they take the time to explain things.

☆ To avoid battles around chores, write your chores on a list and post somewhere you can see them often. Choose to reset and not respond angrily when a parent yells about unfinished chores.

★ It is recommended that teachers take every opportunity in this process to recognize kids for the incredible work of thinking this through and even considering collaboration scenarios with parents.

★ This is also a perfect opportunity to teach children about the possibility of channeling the intense energy of conflict into solutions as a next-level kind of resetting—going beyond a simple letting-go to the purposeful use of the energy of negativity.

GKI ACTIVITIES FOR VERY YOUNG CHILDREN —
TEACHING THE THREE STANDS USING THREE POPULAR CHILDREN'S BOOKS [7]

Caps For Sale
Alexander and the Terrible, Horrible, No Good, Very Bad Day
Thidwick the Big-Hearted Moose

Caps for Sale, by Esphyr Slobodkina, helps young children better understand Stand One.

☆ A peddler loses his caps to a rowdy gang of monkeys. He yells and yells; things escalate between him and the monkeys; and at some point, he is frustrated enough to leaves his cap and turn around. Once he resets himself and stops energizing the monkeys, they give back his caps.

Alexander and the Terrible, Horrible, No Good, Very Bad Day, by Judith Viorst, can be used to teach young children about Stand Two.[8]

☆ On each page, ask kids: What is going right?

Thidwick the Big-Hearted Moose, written by Dr. Seuss, provides an excellent way to teach young kids about Stand Three.

☆ Thidwick wants to help others, so he lets them pile up on his horns. Eventually he can't manage their weight and falls into despair...until he realizes he can shed his own horns and start again. He can reset. Read the book and ask the group: when does he start getting upset? Is there a more effective way to set limits?

NURTURE MY HEART —

This lesson is specifically designed for very young kids to share how and why to use the Nurtured Heart Approach, and to introduce resets to the group. Have a copy of *Nurture My Heart* by Catherine Stafford (available on Amazon.com) on hand.

* Introduce the book by showing the cover and reading the title. Lead a discussion about what students think the word *nurture* means. Link all comments to the understanding of the word. Let students know that the story is about using NHA with children.
* Share that there are places in the story where they will notice rhyming. For the first reading, very young students generally are able to fill in the word *heart* near the end of the story. Pause, place your hand on your heart, and allow them to fill in the word "heart" by saying it all together.
* As you read through the story, be sure to add comments or questions as you check for understanding—especially when resets are being mentioned.

---

[7] These book-related activities were contributed by Yael Walfish, LCSW, Passaic, NJ.
[8] Yael thanks fellow trainer Reuven Rosen for sharing this idea with her.

* When finished with the story, ask students for feedback and comments. You will hear the sweetest comments from your group members!
* Give recognition for paying attention, being focused, following along, sharing, and other qualities you notice.

This story illustrates the way in which Catherine Stafford's wonderful book can be used to introduce NHA to very young children.

I had been asked by a teacher I was coaching to help her teach resets to her challenging and very large Pre-K class. We scheduled a time, and I said I would read a book aloud to her class while using the strategies of NHA. I invited her to participate in the group so that she could experience the energy of what I was doing. She was open, willing, and grateful for the support.

When I showed up in class, she had just finished the opening part of her morning carpet time. I asked the students to form a large circle and to sit on their behinds. From the minute I began the group, I employed Creative Recognitions: I recognized the class for listening to me, sitting all the way down, and being ready for the story.

Within moments of introducing myself, I had occasion to give out a few resets along with recognitions for following those resets. I did not explain anything about resets, I just gave them. Then, I read *Nurture My Heart* to the group. As I read through the story, I found ways to make it interactive. I told the students that if I came across rhyming words, I would pause and they could fill in the rhyming word. I asked questions about the illustrations and what they noticed on each page. Along the way, I gave frequent recognitions for staying quiet, being focused, sitting down, keeping their hands to themselves and showing self-control, responding to my questions, and being great listeners. I gave resets and followed up with more resets where needed, or with recognition when they took the reset and got back on track. The story taught resets, and the learning was reinforced as I modeled them along the way.

— CE

GREATNESS IS MY SUPERPOWER

To support young children in knowing that they possess qualities of greatness.

* Inside the front cover in the book you will find a page titled, **Ways to Expand Learning Using This Book in the Classroom.**
* Use these suggestions; modify to your age group.

Chapter Eight

GREATNESS KIDS ACTIVITIES

CREATED BY NHA TRAINERS

These activities were contributed by amazing educators, therapists, youth program providers, and parents from around the world. Every person who contributed activities to this chapter is a certified Nurtured Heart Approach Advanced Trainer who has been through at least one Certification Training Intensive (CTI) and is actively using and teaching the NHA in their work with youth, families, and others.

Dr. Sally Baas, New Brighton, Minnesota

Dr. Baas is Professor and Director of the Southeast Asian Teacher Program, Hmong Culture and Language Program at Concordia University, St. Paul, MN; she is also a Children's Success Foundation Board Member.

CAPTAIN GREATNESS —

This activity is well suited for young children in camp or group home settings.

* Each day, choose a character quality; have Captain Greatness (clothed in cape and sunglasses) reveal the daily quality at the start of that day.
* At the end of the day, during community time, 10 campers are

recognized across the age spectrum for expressing this quality.

* As these campers are called up to the front, they also receive capes and sunglasses. Captain Greatness capes them up and honors them for showing the character quality of the day.

Lindsay Bingham, MPH, Tucson, AZ

Lindsay's background is in public health education and health promotion. She spends her time managing and collaborating with several health-focused after-school programs, specifically with late-elementary school children; she also teaches a service-based graduate and undergraduate course at the University of Arizona College of Public Health.

KINDNESS CHAIN: FOSTERING COMMUNITY AND INNER WEALTH

In an activity lasting about 40 minutes, youth build a chain of recognitions about fellow youth, including observations about others' strengths. They also write recognitions about themselves to encourage positive self-esteem. All of the recognitions are incorporated into a paper chain as a visual representation of the group's kindness and interconnectedness.

* Gather colored pencils, tape, strips of colored paper (prepare beforehand: cut into strips approximately 2"x11" – for younger children, write short prompts on some of the strips to guide them in the activity).
* Seat the group in a circle, with everyone facing inward toward the center of the circle.
* Complete a brief discussion with the children asking questions such as: "What does it mean to be kind to others?" and "How do we show people kindness?"
* Examples could be doing a favor for someone, saying something nice to someone, holding the door open, using good manners.
* "What kinds of things can we say to people to show them kindness?"
* "How does it make you feel when people are kind to you?"
* Ask the youth to think about a time that someone was kind to them and to give examples. Also, ask the youth to think about a time that they showed kindness and encourage them to share those experiences with the group.
* Pass out the strips of paper and allow children to write recognitions

about the other youth in the group using the prompted strips or by creating their own.

* If you worry that some young people may not receive enough recognition, have students/youth sit in a circle during the activity and write about the person to their left.
* Examples of prompted strips:

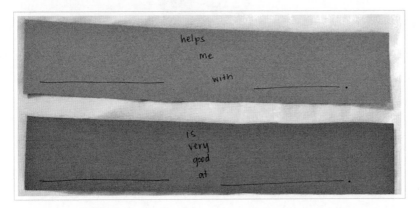

For self-acknowledgements, a prompted strip might read:

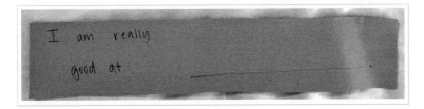

* As the youth finish each recognition, have them read the recognitions out loud to the youth at whom the recognition is directed.
* As the youth complete each recognition, use tape to close the strips into loops and begin interlocking the strips, creating a paper chain of recognitions (photo example provided below).
* When the youth have completed 2-3 recognitions each, ask the group to come back together for a discussion related to self-esteem and worth. Remind the students of the discussion at the beginning about the importance of being kind to others and introduce the youth to the idea of why it's important to be kind to one's self.

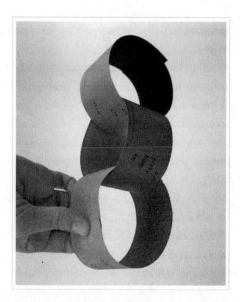

* Then, ask youth about the things that they are best at or things they take pride in. Encourage them to share those things with the group.
* Have each child take a strip of paper and write a compliment about themselves. For example: "I am proud of my grades at school," "I am really good at basketball."
* Youth can be given guidance for how to "notch up" recognitions to themselves and others: "I have super-intelligence," or "I am incredibly athletic."
* Add all remaining strips to the paper chain.
* Bring the children back together for a final wrap-up. Bring their attention to the length of the chain and the number of recognitions that were added. Ask the following questions:

  ☆ What did you learn from this activity?
  ☆ How did it make you feel when you heard some of the recognitions that others wrote about you?
  ☆ Why is it important to show kindness to others?
  ☆ Why is it important to show kindness to yourself?

* Hang the paper chain in a visible place as a reminder of the importance of being kind to one another.
* Complete the activity by emphasizing the following takeaway points:

☆ It's easy to be kind to one another! Just a few nice words or a kind action can make a big difference. It can be more challenging – and that much more important – to be kind to yourself! Remember to take pride in the things you ARE and recognize yourself every day.

☆ By being kind, we can create a community of inner wealth that links us together as shown by our kindness chain!

* Display the Kindness Chain at the end of the activity so youth can read their recognitions often. Each week, have a time for youth to add recognitions of themselves to the chain. You can also welcome them to add recognitions of themselves and others during breaks or when they think of HOW they show their greatness.

Meghan Blakey, Spring, Texas
Meghan is a school counselor at Benfer Elementary School.

WHAT'S GOING RIGHT SCAVENGER HUNT —

A fun way to support young children in catching their peers in greatness!Pass out a sheet with the following information:

* A blank for students' names.
* Directions:

Find these people or situations. Put their first name by the statement. When the teacher asks for you to share, tell your classmates what you saw them doing that shows their greatness, then have them each initial your paper where you've written their name.

Find someone who is:

_____ 1. Quietly listening
_____ 2. Taking notes
_____ 3. Not talking
_____ 4. Smiling
_____ 5. Not hitting
_____ 6. Ready to go with materials
_____ 7. Raising their hand to talk

8. Keeping their eyes on the teacher
9. Sitting in seat
10. Waiting patiently

Bonus: write 5 things you notice that are going right.

* Have students keep track for a class period or a whole day. Take time for students to go to those they wrote on their sheet, share appreciation, and get their initials.

DeLisa Boyd, Ballantyne, North Carolina

DeLisa Boyd is Chief Executive Officer of the GEMS Network and Diamond Ambassadors. She has also worked as CEO of a school-based Debutante program, as an Adoption Specialist for the New Jersey Department of Children and Families Adoption Operation Central Office, as a Child Protection Investigator/Forensic Specialist for the New Jersey Department of Children and Families, and as the Union County Children's Mobile Response and Stabilization System Clinician and Psychiatric Rehabilitation Work Unit Coordinator at Mount Sinai Hospital in New York City.

EMOTIONALLY NUTRITIOUS WORD BINGO

A game inspired by an old favorite!

* Create bingo cards for your group containing 24 words (if needed, consult the list on pages 53-55 for ideas) and a blank square, situated on a 5x5 grid. Ensure that no two cards are identical.
* Keep a list of the words you used on the cards.
* Players can play with one or multiple cards.
* Emotionally nutritious words are read out from the list; players mark words that match those on their cards.
* The first player(s) who complete five words in a diagonal, horizontal, or vertical row are winners.
* When one or more players shout "Bingo!" the game stops and the words are verified.
* Winner(s) stand from their seats and engage peers with as many of the nutritious words in their bingo sequence as possible, giving present-time examples of those qualities in those being engaged/energized: "Celeste,

you are a great example of a good friend, because you are **committed** to being a **great listener,** you are **authentic,** and you are always **attentive.**"
* Give a prize – if you don't think that a chance to energize peers is prize enough! – to the winner(s).

Allison Brooks, Sacramento, California
Allie is a Lower Grade Curriculum Specialist and mentor.

VALENTINE ACKNOWLEDGMENTS

In this activity, children create one special valentine that richly energizes one of their classmates.

* Put all students' names into a hat. Have each person draw one name and tell them that this person will be their secret Valentine.
* Have each student think about the greatness of the person they chose, make a Valentine card, and write acknowledgements of their greatness on the back.
* On Valentine's Day, everyone enjoys a potluck together and exchanges Valentine cards. One at a time, each student goes to the front of the room and reads their Valentine aloud to the group.
* Teacher can also distribute hearts to each student – each with qualities of greatness they've written about that student.

BIRTHDAY GREATNESS BOOK

An idea for celebrating birthdays through amplifying greatness:

* Sometime before a student's birthday, have the class brainstorm the birthday kid's greatness. Make a list on the whiteboard.
* Using the list as inspiration, have each child write an acknowledgment about the birthday person and draw a picture for that person on an individual page. Bind the pages into a book.
* During the child's birthday celebration, read the book aloud; have each student who has contributed stand while their contribution is read.

Bobbi Claytor, Harpers Ferry, West Virginia
Bobbi is a 4th grade teacher at Eagle School Intermediate in Martinsburg, West Virginia.

STAFF GREATNESS POSTERS —

Bobbi conjured up the idea of creating Greatness Posters for staff members who have touched their lives, then surprising those staff members by posting the poster on their door, desk, or classroom wall where they'll see it the next time they come in.

GREATNESS POST-ITS —

A good end-of-year activity.

* Pass out Post-It notes, giving each child in the group the same number of Post-It sheets as there are total children in the group.
* Have the children write the name of every other child in the room on one of their Post-Its, then write a word or statement about each of their classmates' greatness on that Post-It.
* Have each child give their note to the child they are written about.
* Each child has the opportunity to read the notes, and to then arrange them on a poster-sized piece of construction paper.
* Have the posters laminated if possible to send home as a greatness decoration!

Danielle Cossett, LCSW, Corrales, New Mexico
Danielle is Clinical Director at a community mental health center in Albuquerque. These activities can be done in large group, small group, pairs, or in a family therapy context.

EMOTIONALLY NUTRITIOUS WORDS ACTIVITY —

For this activity, have a list of emotionally nutritious words on hand.

* Ask participants to review the list privately and to identify two to three qualities of greatness they know they already are, and to reflect on evidence that they possess these qualities.

* One participant shares with their partner/the group:

  ☆ Qualities they are, with evidence.
  ☆ The one quality (of the three) they would like to grow, and why they would like to grow it.

* Another participant then reflects back to the other person the qualities of greatness shared, including the evidence; and the quality the other person shared that they are striving for.
* That second participant then offers evidence that the person sharing already does possess the latter quality.

The intent of this activity is to providing proof/evidence that the person sharing is already the quality to which they aspire. Simply hearing the person share about the qualities they have and wish to grow should be adequate for the other person to recognize ways in which the latter quality is already abundantly visible.

GREATNESS CARDS ACTIVITY

Have on hand a stack of index cards with one quality of greatness word on each card. This activity works for pairs or groups.

* Have players randomly choose a card/quality of greatness.
* The person who picks the card reflects on evidence that they already demonstrate; and/or it could be a quality that they may not have considered for themselves yet.
* Partners/others in the group share their own quality and evidence they see.
* Facilitator may need to guide and assist participants with language of energizing.
* Can be an emotionally vulnerable experience; it's smart to have tissue handy.

Cindy Cummons LCSW, St. Louisville, Ohio
Cindy works as a Clinical Social Worker in private practice at Bridgewater Counseling and Consulting, Ltd.

THE GREAT PUMPKIN –

A great big pumpkin dubbed (of course) "The Great Pumpkin" helps kids and leaders in a therapy group to record qualities of greatness seen during group time around the Halloween season.

* At the end of each group session, kids and leaders write on the pumpkin with permanent marker the greatness qualities they saw during the group.
* Additions can be made throughout the month of October.

Achala Matthew Godino, Boston, Massachusetts
Achala Matthew is a Primary Guide at Alighieri Montessori School in East Boston.

CIRCLE TIME GREATNESS RECOGNITIONS –

During regular circle time, this teacher's third, fourth, and fifth graders take time to do a Greatness Circle.

* Children and teachers offer observations of greatness: for example, "I noticed that Camila and Lorna cleaned up the big paint spill. They showed cooperation."
* The children usually have so many 'greatnesses' to share that they don't have time for all of them on any one day!

Sarah How and Kaia Hassel, Fargo, ND
Kaia Hassel is a 5ᵗʰ Grade Teacher at Westside Elementary in Fargo, ND. Sarah How is a school psychologist in Fargo.

THE I AM BOARD –

The first I AM Board, inspired by the Nurtured Heart Approach, was created in Kaia Hassel's 5th grade classroom. The goal was to introduce the definitions of many emotionally rich vocabulary words and to shift the culture of the classroom.

* Make magnetic name tags for each student as well as every staff member and teacher. Place them all together on one side of a magnetic classroom

bulletin board so that they can easily be found by students.

* Make magnetic versions of as many qualities of greatness as can fit on your bulletin board. Post them in a visually appealing way across the board.
* Write "I AM…" in the center of the board.
* Ensure that students know how to give experiential and proactive recognitions, with evidence to support (not simply saying "You are…").
* When students arrive at school, they have a name of another student on a sticky note on their desk: for explanation's sake, let's say Student A has been assigned Student B.
* When Student A observes a quality of greatness in Student B, they go up to the I Am Board and select Student B's name from the list. Student A places Student B's name next to the quality being recognized and writes evidence on the Post-It note they received with Student B's name on it.
* In Sarah and Kaia's classroom, the qualities recognized in students are also written on the back of their name tags.

A few fun variations:

* Feature a single greatness quality for the week; see how often and in how many ways students can be recognized for that particular quality.
* Create a video in black and white with students claiming a word off the I AM board. Then video, in color, students stating the word and then giving irrefutable evidence that they possess that quality.
* At the end of the day, have one student sit in the middle of the class, while classmates reference the I AM board to give proactive or experiential recognitions. A student can keep notes on the computer so that the student can have the paper to reference in the future.
* Have students invite support staff – counselors, kitchen staff, aides, or others – to come and be a part of the I AM board recognitions.
* Use white board markers to write on the desks of student with greatness words from the I AM board.
* For younger students, try assigning a "Greatness Spy" whose job it is to call out greatness throughout the day. Having the I AM board allows them to keep in mind things to see in others. They can also have assigned times to add to the board.
* Teachers can use this instead of the clip-up/clip-down chart. Instead of moving students up or down, they call out students' greatness on the I

AM board. They can ask students to share ideas about why their name was moved, or call them out on the greatness they see.

Dana Kasowski, Wahpeton, Iowa, and Louisa Triandis, LCSW, Solana Beach, California

Louisa works as a School Social Worker and counselor. Dana is an elementary school special education teacher. They both enjoy leading groups in making "Greatness Gems."

GREATNESS GEMS

For this fun craft activity, order clear flat marbles from Amazon.com. When planning the activity, include time for gems to dry overnight.

* Distribute several clear flat marbles to each student.
* Distribute pieces of scrapbook paper cut in one-inch circles. Have all group members write qualities of their greatness, using colorful marker or colored pencil.
* Have group members then decoupage the paper circles onto the small clear marbles, creating "greatness gems."
* Allow a full day to dry.
* The gems can be sent home or given to administrators and teachers, who then hand them out to students and staff.
* Dana's students love to pick out gems for friends and teachers and hand-deliver them. Her students will also take special requests for gems with particular words on them.

Kids take great pride in making and distributing these gems!

Hitomi Kawai, Shizuoka, Japan

Hitomi works in the Sogetsu Counseling Center as a counselor for children, teens, and adults.

FRUIT BASKET ACTIVITY

First, put enough chairs for the whole group in a big circle, leaving one chair out so that one person – "it" – has to stand.

* Have that one person stand in the middle of the circle.
* The person in the middle shares a reason why they are great: "I have the greatness of having fun while playing this game!" or "I have the greatness of courage because I am speaking in front of everyone right now!"
* If those who are sitting down have the same quality, they have to rise and find a new chair. Whichever person can't find a new chair is now "it."
* If "It" calls "FRUIT BASKET!" everyone has to move.

Jennifer Kelley, Syracuse, New York

Jennifer worked as a social worker for approximately 20 years, working with individuals with mental health issues. She also worked the last few years as a grant writer for an inclusive preschool. For the past two years, she has been homeschooling her oldest daughter and teaching about greatness at their homeschooling co-op. Her youngest child goes to public school and she continues to try to spread NHA each year to her team. Both of her children – who have special needs – love NHA and she is eternally grateful for its introduction into their lives.

GREATNESS PROFILE

The class works on this over a period of two weeks, then those who want to can share their profile with the whole class. Each kid hangs theirs above their locker in the hallway for all the school to see.

Greatness Profile

Name:_____

Some of My Interests: _____
_____
_____

Something People Don't Know About Me : _____
_____
_____

Something That Makes Me Different: _____
_____
_____

My Best Talent Is... _____
_____
_____

Josh Kuersten, M.Ed., and Rebecca Stevens, Chico, California
Josh is a behavior specialist and Rebecca is a fourth-grade teacher.

ENERGIZING OBJECTS —

This activity gives group members a chance to practice energizing language in an unintimidating way.

* If numbers provide, form small groups.
* Provide each group with objects: a chair, a lamp, a box, and other everyday items that most of us take for granted day to day.
* Have group members take turns practicing recognizing one object at a time in their groups.
* Rotate the objects between groups, so that every person in the room has a chance to recognize every object.
* Recognize the children along the way for creativity of their recognitions.
* When all objects have been recognized by each group, have group members share out some of their recognitions for each object.
* Close with recognitions for the entire group and their participation.

Kay Lara, Madison, Wisconsin
Kay is the owner of Lera Wellness & Care, LLC.

GREATNESS MOMENT —

Simple, powerful, and useful for any adult, anywhere, any time a group is together.

* At any random time, stop and ask group members, "What's great in this moment?"
* Let one to three people share, depending on how much time is available. Ask each person how it feels to share something great before moving on.
* This can be used in calm and focused environments but is even more powerful in not-so-calm environments.

GREATNESS CIRCLE VARIATIONS

Use Greatness Circles to:

* Welcome back someone who is coming back into the group after a meltdown.
* Focus on sharing observations about people who are using what has been taught in the weekly lesson (for example, recognitions, resetting, or not giving energy to negativity).
* Share what greatness group members have seen happening outside of group time (mom, dad, at karate, at the store...).

GRATITUDE PARTY

In this activity, the class, group, or family works to accrue enough 'gratitude points' to earn a party.

* Points are earned whenever a participant hears someone stating a message of gratitude to someone else, followed by the reason for that gratitude. For example: "Thanks a bunch for working quietly at our table during Writer's Workshop. You helped me stay focused and relaxed during our writing time. You're respectful!"
* Decide how many points are needed to earn a Gratitude Party – keep track with a jar, score marks, or other creative method – and have your party once the group's goal is reached!

Kandy Luty, M.Ed., BHT, Phoenix, Arizona
Kandy is a Statewide Curriculum and Youth Education Manager with the Family Involvement Center, a social services organization.

GREATNESS BIRTHDAY CELEBRATION

Kandy creatively celebrates birthdays with greatness recognitions.

* Those with birthdays in the current month receive a heart every day of that month, with evidence of their greatness written on it.

GREATNESS PHOTO OP —

Take a photo of each group member in front of a poster describing their qualities of greatness.

* Have the rest of the group create the poster with space for the person's head so that all greatness qualities are visible in the photo.

Travis Peterson, North Dakota
Travis is a school counselor at Jefferson Elementary School in Valley City, ND. He serves K-3rd grade students.

GREATNESS CONES —

Students make mini-traffic cones with words of recognition printed on them. When a quality of greatness is observed in a student, pause with teaching (leading). Recognize the student verbally and place a cone in front of that student. You can also give students/participants the ability to place the cone in front of their peers and give a recognition.

Lynda Skinner Pirtle, Tucson, AZ
Lynda is co-founder of SkillfullyAware™, an organization specializing in teaching mindfulness to children.

In her work with children, Lynda, focuses on activities that raise what she calls *the three transcendentals:* beauty, truth and goodness.

* First, teach kids about their brains. See Dan Siegel's article at mindful. org, "How to Teach Your Kids About the Brain," for a simple and concise way to teach the basics.[9] This helps kids (and adults) recognize their brains' natural negative attentional bias.
* This can be a lesson all by itself for one day. Lynda uses it as a baseline teaching; it involves teaching young people to notice their own thoughts, first – which helps to support the reset.

Next, teach the Mindfulness/EQ/NHA exercise. This can be done in one day or over three days, depending on time permitted:

* Explore how different emotions feel, with eyes open or closed.
* See how they feel inside when you slowly read these words: happy, sad, excited, mad, stressed, bored, loving, anxious, worried, scared, jealous, quiet, peaceful, silly, joy.
* Ask the group: can you feel the difference?
* Then, ask the group whether they can recognize at least one strong emotion they felt today. It may be anger, excitement, or joy.
* Ask them to drop into feeling the emotion in their bodies. What does it feel like? Butterflies, a swirly feeling? Have them write down how it feels.
* Then, have them drop into how their faces feel when they are happy; into how their bellies feel when they are upset. Ask them how their muscles feel when they are angry. In their writing, have them try to connect the dots between sensations and emotions.
* Have group members name at least one difficult emotion from their day. Encourage them to remember to *name* emotions whenever they can, especially when they are difficult.
* Let them know that paying attention to and naming the feeling can take its power away: "Name it to tame it."
* Ask group members: What emotion did you name? How did it feel in your body?

---

[9] https://www.mindful.org/how-to-teach-your-kids-about-the-brain/

Here is where the NHA is woven in: with an invitation to consider what attributes or positive characteristics were required to do this exercise. Ask them:

* What skills did you used to do this exercise? What did you have to do? Have them write a list and take shout-outs of examples. (Examples of what kids and teens have responded: determination, observation, noticing, dedication, paying attention, focusing on my mind or body, organizing my notes, persistence, understanding.)
* After group members make their positive attributes/skills list, remind them that all of these attributes are within them and can be accessed at any time. Invite them to pull this list out and look at them any time they need support in accessing their greatness.

MINDFULNESS FOR HAPPINESS USING NHA

A mindfulness exercise to help youth feel into memories of moments of greatness. Lead youth through the following meditation:

* Close your eyes or cast your eyes downward.
* Remember a time when you helped someone else feel happy.
* What inspired you to help this person? What did you do to create happiness/joy/excitement in them? Perhaps you simply smiled at someone.
* Remember a wonderful moment like that. Bring it to mind. What did you notice? What did you hear yourself saying? What did they say to you?
* Notice how it feels to hold this memory of sharing happiness/joy. Notice how it feels now in your body.
* Now, gently open your eyes or bring your focus back. Take a moment and write down the positive attributes that were required to bring this happiness to someone. (Words Lynda has seen: kindness, caring, sharing, trying to help someone feel better, wanting to share joy, noticing someone was sad and cheering them up, changing negative feelings into positive ones.)
* Have the kids review their lists and remind them that all of these positive attributes are within them and each of us. Remind them that they had to make a conscious/intentional choice to do what they did.
* Talk to them briefly about the power of choice and how it can impact our days.

* Ask them for examples from throughout the day that show they have the power of choice. What comes out of them is truly amazing.

A final recommendation from Lynda is to check out the website of the Ann Williams Group[10] for craft activities that meld well with the NHA. The Empower Poster Kit and the Family Bowl are excellent options where time permits.

Rachael Roche, Bremmerton, Washington
Rachael is an Early Learning Child Development Coach.

NHA BUCKET ACTIVITY

This is a yearlong activity that works best in a school setting.

* Create a poster featuring a large bucket that can be "filled" with stickers. Post on a wall of the classroom.
* Demonstrate how the bucket works by giving recognitions to students and handing a sticker to each student being recognized.
* At the end of the recognition and sticker giving, have the students place their sticker in the class bucket. Explain that the intention for the year is to fill the class bucket by "tattling" to you about classmates' greatness.
* When they "tattle," their classmate receives a sticker to add to the bucket.
* Make clear that students may not ask for appreciations to receive stickers. The object is to *give* appreciations.

Lyla Tyler LMFT, RPT-S, Sacramento CA
Lyla is an LMFT and Registered Play Therapy Supervisor. She owns a counseling center called Kid Counseling Sacramento. She is also an Advanced NHA trainer who loves using play therapy techniques to teach NHA to families and children.

RESET STICKS

This activity teaches family members coping skills useful for resetting.

* Gather supplies: pick-up sticks (find the jumbo version Lyla prefers at

---

[10]www.annwilliamsgroup.com

Amazon.com) and paper and pen.

* Gather the family on the playroom floor and explain that we all get upset and need to learn to reset ourselves. Ask each family member about something that makes them angry, normalize the feeling, and stress the importance of learning to reset.
* Explain how to play pick-up sticks: drop the sticks on the floor, then try to pick up a stick without moving any other sticks. If they do this successfully, they think of a way they can reset using their senses. They'll know which sense to think about based on the color stick they've picked up:

  ☆ Red sticks = using your mouth to reset (to talk to someone, ask for help, sing a song, drink some water)
  ☆ Blue sticks = using your eyes to reset (to close them and meditate, or to look at a picture book)
  ☆ Green sticks = using your hands or feet to reset (use my hands to write in my journal, or my feet to go for a run)
  ☆ Yellow sticks = using your nose to reset (use my nose to smell a rose in the garden, or to take a deep breath)

* As they think of ideas, energize the greatness of those ideas and write them down for the family to post at home and add to.
* Encourage them to try the different ways to reset and report back which work best for each of them. The person with the most sticks is the winner!

GREATNESS CRAYON ART

An individual art activity that helps kids and teens recognize their greatness. Lyla has used this with kids and teens in individual therapy sessions and also when meeting with a child and parent.

* Gather supplies: canvas (Lyla uses 5x7), crayons, blow dryer, glue gun, fork, oven mitt, paper to cover table, big piece of cardboard to keep area from getting too messy.
* Have the child list some things that they are great at. Have the parent help identify their greatness. Examples are: I'm a great friend, I help my mom with chores, I am creative, I am kind to my brother.

* Another fun thing to do prior to doing this activity is to have the child ask family, friends and teachers to list three great things about them. This will help them identify their positive traits more easily and reinforce the use of Stand Two outside of the therapy session or group time.
* For each positive trait, have them choose a crayon. The child breaks the crayon to show how great they are and removes the paper from the crayon. They use the glue gun to glue each crayon to the top of the canvas.
* Now the fun begins: They use the hair dryer to melt the crayons. Have them use the fork to hold any crayon that breaks loose from the glue and have them wear the mitt on the hand that holds the canvas.
* Watch together as the crayons melt and run down the page, making a beautiful piece of art symbolizing their greatness.
* Have them take it home to hang on the wall to remind them of their greatness!

Gaylene Vickers, Greene, Iowa
Gaylene works as a caseworker doing in-home support for families with children.

PUZZLE RECOGNITIONS

* Gaylene has worked with a variety of activities using puzzles; she has blended and simplified them to an activity for anywhere from two to 24 people. The smaller the group, the more recognitions each person gives and gets. She has especially liked using this activity for home family visits to enhance their ability to use emotionally nutritious language, give recognitions and evidence, and promote increased Inner Wealth. The language of NHA can be a challenge for some; this allows practice in a controlled setting.
* Use a 24-piece puzzle. On the back of each piece, using capital letters, write a letter from the alphabet. Omit two letters used least often to start words (X, Y, or Z are good ones) so there are 24 letters being used.
* Either assemble the puzzle before you meet; or, in the case of in-home services, have the family complete it. Once the puzzle is completed, point out that there is a letter on each piece, and that you will now take turns un-assembling the puzzle one piece at a time.
* If you wish to model the activity, you might strategically place a letter in the top right-hand corner with a quality that you wish to energize in

the group you are working with. For example: you could place the letter "C" in the top right-hand corner. "The letter C...Cooperation. I see the entire family/group cooperating by joining together in this activity. That shows a commitment to making change."

* When working with a family, start with the OLDEST player first. They are most likely to quickly grasp the concept of giving recognitions supported by present-moment evidence. They choose a piece and energize the group for a quality that starts with that letter.

* It is your job to help guide, provide support and encourage, and to offer up additional recognitions as needed to build confidence in using the new language as the family plays the game.

* Provide clarity that negative comments are not allowed. Reset the group if someone says something negative; ask them to rephrase. Keep track of any negative words that do emerge. These words tend to be the "default" or negative labels that have been given to the person who uses them.

* After focusing on the 24 positives, have a conversation about the list of negative words. Ask: Can they be looked at differently? For example, if someone used the word "stubborn," ask: "Is stubborn bad?" Invite the group to come up with another word that reflects the positive aspects of stubbornness. Point out that to make something happen, one has to be determined, has to be focused on a specific outcome, and needs patience to make something happen.

Yael Walfish, LCSW, Passaic, New Jersey
Yael is a licensed clinical social worker (LCSW) who works with families.

NURTURED HEART *BAT MITZVAH* —

Yael's incredible creativity with NHA led her to weave Nurtured Heart activities throughout her daughter's *bat mitzvah* celebration.

* When people walked into the celebration, they found scrapbooking pages for Yael's daughter, with art supplies including positive stickers: "You got this," "Kindness changes everything," and so on. Everyone got involved with a scrapbooking project that was filled with positivity.

* Bar and bat mitzvahs are about the transformation from childhood to adulthood, and there is usually some acknowledgement of the challenges and fears that come with growing up. This isn't out of alignment with

NHA – this Approach is not about being unfailingly positive by ignoring life's difficulties but wraps in embracing risk and challenge and finding ways to celebrate their gifts and beauty. The theme of the event was "darkness," and nods to this theme included cookies with sunglasses on them...but also a more serious acknowledgement of darkness when it was time for the bat mitzvah's speech in front of the entire group.

* In her speech, she spoke of darkness that prevents people from seeing what is right about themselves and what others need.
* She also spoke about the greatness of her great-grandmother, for whom she was named, and said the most important thing she had known about her was that she always had a positive attitude.
* After her speech, the entire group took a photograph with sunglasses on and another with sunglasses off – to actualize the darkness and light that are possible.
* Another activity the group enjoyed together during the gathering was decorating ceramic mugs with paint pens. People made mugs for themselves featuring their own qualities of greatness: creative, smart, responsible, and so on.

Janet Waller, New Rochelle, New York
Janet is a recently retired elementary school teacher.

END OF YEAR GREATNESS GIFTS

Janet asked her 5th grade class – the first one she taught after starting to learn the Nurtured Heart Approach – to make greatness gifts for each other at the end of the year. The gift: a booklet for each child, filled with positive recognitions from each member of the class.

* Gather materials: a photo of each student, a 12x18 piece of construction paper for each student (folded over into a booklet shape), and a class list for each student with a long space after each name (enough to write a sentence).
* Have each student glue their photo to the front of the booklet.
* Ask the kids to each write a positive recognition for each person in the class – a recognition of a special quality they really appreciate about each person. Allow plenty of time and space for this part of the activity and be available to support students in staying positive

with their comments (resetting them where needed and giving them positive recognitions as they complete the activity). Have them sign their own name after each recognition.

* Have students cut out the sentence strips and go around the room to glue them into the booklets of their classmates.
* Students LOVE reading the recognitions and receiving these gifts. Some ideas of greatness to recognize during the activity:

  ☆ Giving the gift of beautiful, heartfelt words
  ☆ Being thoughtful
  ☆ Following directions even though they seem complicated at first
  ☆ Staying focused
  ☆ Carefully gluing in their sentences, leaving room for others' contributions
  ☆ Showing appreciation for each other and for receiving the gift of words
  ☆ Being generous with their expressions of appreciation
  ☆ Persevering even though this takes quite a bit of time and energy

PUBLISHING PARTIES —

Janet had a tradition of unit-end Publishing Parties for years, even before she learned about the NHA. This would give her a chance to publish students' writing and allow them to share their work with an appreciative audience. This is a powerful way to celebrate all the qualities of greatness it takes to go through the process of writing – and it builds motivation and community. The finished product shows students, in a very tangible way, that they have accomplished something that they can feel proud of.

* Ensure that every student has their published piece of writing to share and a lined sheet of paper with their name and the title of their piece of writing at the top. Have students post them around the room.
* Invite another class, parents, administrators, and other staff members to come in to take part in the Publishing Party.
* When guests arrive, welcome them and give a short introduction about the writing the group has been working on and what they have accomplished in this area of learning. For example: when Janet's class did narrative writing, they were learning to write a small seed story, not a big watermelon topic; to think about the heart of the story; to choose

powerful words; to "explode a moment" and to craft leads and endings.

* Invite everyone to walk around the room and read each piece of writing, and to then sign the paper and write a detailed comment, telling the student something they had done well in their writing. Provide examples: "Don't just say, 'I liked your writing,'" say, "I liked the part when you told about going fishing with your grandpa. I could really picture everything you did together."

* Help folks recognize the qualities of greatness it takes to go through the writing process – qualities like being able to choose an idea (decisiveness, trust in one's self), learning to have a conference with a teacher and with a peer (collaboration), willingness to use a mentor text and learn from authors and other student writers (openness to wise feedback and guidance), trying something new (courage), writing for a certain amount of time each day (discipline), willingness to re-read and revise (patience, perseverance), asking for help (vulnerability, trust), offering help (helpfulness, kindness, wisdom)…and the list goes on.

* Provide refreshments for just your class – a special time can be shared after the guests leave for just the featured writers of the day.

I-MESSAGES

This is another one Janet learned about way before she knew the Nurtured Heart Approach; its power grew as she saw how it could bring out children's greatness in the area of conflict resolution. While teaching fourth grade, she saw her class go through a time of discord where students were not being kind to each other, were tattling, and were not getting along. She went to the school social worker, who visited the classroom to teach students about the use of I-Messages to solve interpersonal conflicts. It was so helpful that since then, Janet made a habit of introducing this tool to children during the first week of school and coaching them in using it throughout the year.

* There are three parts of an I-Message. They are:

1. **"I feel…"** The child shares their emotion: frustrated, upset, angry, disappointed, sad – whatever is real for them in the moment.
2. **"Because you…"** The child shares, factually, what the other person did to cause them to have this emotion. This is not about finger-pointing, storytelling, or blaming, but is exclusively about naming

the facts of the situation that were upsetting.

3. **"And I want…"** The child then gets to share how they want the other person to repair the harm their actions have caused (whether intentionally or not). For example: "I want you to give me back my pencil" or "I want you to stop calling me names."

* Introduce these ideas to students, then give them a chance to role-play with made-up scenarios (one child pretends to do something offensive and the other gives an I-Message).

* Here's the part that brings this into the territory of the Nurtured Heart Approach: be on the lookout for every opportunity to energize children for doing this well. Being able to work through conflict using I-Statements requires emotional intelligence, vulnerability, assertiveness, self-respect, compassion, honesty, and many, many other important qualities of greatness.

* To avoid focusing on the negative, stay away from any kind of "crime scene investigation" (CSI) or delving into any kind of "he said/she said" storytelling. I-messages brilliantly shift the focus to the present moment and give students an opportunity to problem-solve and acknowledge their own emotions and boundaries.

* It is powerful to energize one student for being assertive and the other for listening and admitting what they did and being willing to solve the problem.

* If a child is not ready to apologize, thank them for listening to the other child; let them know you will be checking back in later once they have had time to consider how they would most like to mend things with their peer.

Dr. Paula Wick, Madison, WI
Paula Wick describes herself simply as an "educator and energizer"!

EYE-POPPING AWESOME —

When Dr. Wick first read the expression "You're eye-popping awesome!" in an NHA book, *The Inner Wealth Initiative (2007)*, she could not imagine herself saying it. This alternative to saying "thank you" seemed much too saccharine for her style. Finding this EyePopper squeezable soft foam shooter from Hog Wild changed her tune in a big way.

That's right: Dr. Wick took to blasting eyeballs and accompanying recognitions across the room to fourth and fifth graders! This toy helped keep her mind and heart open to possibilities... also eye-popping awesome. At some point, she had students decorate more eyes as a celebration of greatness.

BREATHE! —

Incorporating mindfulness practices into her teaching was another complement to NHA that Dr. Wick needed to grow into. A few ways she was able to slow herself and students down included props that drew attention to breathing and gentle stretching.

* She tried using a Slinky and a Hoberman Sphere (see photo) to help students visualize the length and depth of inbreaths and outbreaths, expanding and contracting the toys in time with slow, sustained breaths.
* She also modeled by taking her own breaths, then asking the kids to join in: "Let's just take a few breaths together...inhale...exhale..."

POSITIVE AND NEGATIVE ENERGY ACTIVITY —

Dr. Wick used a tool designed for illustrating fractions and percentages to invite students to help take responsibility for the energy of the classroom.

* Two interlocking paper plates (see image) became their gauge for

showing how much positive and negative energy was perceived at any given time.

* In addition, students collected data reflecting the climate of the room as they pursued the goal of six positives to one negative interaction.
* Support students in continuing to feel into the subtleties of negativity and being able to reset around it through acknowledgments for their growing skills as you witness them.
* Acknowledge often the growing greatness and skill you witness in your students: the loving kindness, supportiveness, collaboration, and other wise and wonderful qualities you see emerging and growing in the realm of positivity.

MIND JARS

Small jars containing glitter glue and water in a jar serve as a reminder to settle ourselves.

* The colorful cloud of glitter in the shaken jar illustrates the dysregulated brain, or amygdala hijack, that can happen to anyone at any time.
* The natural settling of the glitter when the jar is still illustrates the brain and body calming themselves.
* The mind jar also sparks conversation and helps normalize the need for reset strategies.

Visuals have supported Dr. Wick's learning of the NHA.

* On occasion, she painted just one thumbnail silver, symbolizing a mirror that would remind her to start with herself – to attend to how she responds to circumstances, events and relational energy rather than thinking of the NHA as something to implement to change others.

* In trainings for adults learning NHA, she sometimes will don a referee jersey and grab a clipboard and pom-pom to explain her role in implementing the NHA with children.
* She describes herself as a referee with the job of clarifying and implementing the rules in a fair, un-energized way; as a coach, responsible for teaching and inspiring greatness; and as part of the cheering squad, always looking for what's right. Dr. Wick keeps these objects hung in her classroom to support her efforts.

This warning to "Mind the Gap" is posted in U.K. train stations to alerts rail passengers to be cautious of the spatial gap between the train door and the station platform.

* Dr. Wick keeps this sign posted in her room to remind herself to pause and find the space between feeling an emotion and responding to it.
* It helps her slow down as well as to appreciate those who already choose wisely in the throes of chaos.

Neils Wright, Oroville, California

Neils works as an English teacher at Marysville Community Day School.

WAYS TO ADAPT COMMON GAMES FOR USE IN GREATNESS KIDS INITIATIVES —

* Rather than "losing" or being "out," have players give another player a recognition.
* You can also use giving or receiving recognitions as a prize/reward for winning at a game.
* Encourage recognitions for fairness and good sportsmanship.

GREATS AND APPRECIATIONS —

This activity is a wonderful opportunity for children to practice being present to energy and consciously using it to fuel greatness. It's a great activity to wrap up the end of a week and works well on Friday afternoons.

* Ask participants to recall something great (an event) and an appreciation of someone from the week.
* Following the event and the appreciation of someone, have each person share the greatness demonstrated by themselves or others for one of their appreciations. Have everyone share one at a time and encourage all participants to notice the energy of the appreciations and to take the energy in as fuel for the weekend ahead.
* For example: recently, Neils' "great of the week" event was that his mom made it to her cancer appointment this week. His appreciation was for Celeste for creating and supporting a greatly appreciated and needed fundraiser for NHA trainers impacted by the Camp Fire.

* Neils then chose to focus on his mother's oncology appointments in order to share his greatness during the event. He shared that in the moments of what turned out to be his mother's last such appointment, he was the greatness of dedication to his mother, of compassion, and of willingness to make things right for her. He was the greatness of deep love and kindness and of putting his mother's wishes first.

I made a phone call to Neils this morning to ask him about the greatness he demonstrated in supporting his mother to be at her oncology appointment during the week he had mentioned. I was calling for information about a past event, yet the call quickly turned into a powerful conversation where he was able to identify the greatness he is today.

Although during our call he was in a tough, emotional space around his mother's illness, he was able to dig deep to share the greatness of being the kind of son he is able to be right now. His words were so energetically heartfelt, honest, and loving that I was able to take the energy of his sharing and to use that energy as an opportunity to recognize him. I appreciated him for having the intention of being present with his mother in a way that is showing her great love and support during this difficult time, and giving himself the gift of knowing that he is holding a level of presence in the midst of these moments that he can treasure forever. I shared that in my own life, I've been able to revisit moments of being intentionally present with my own father during his last days.

Even though Neils and I were on a phone call, we were both profoundly speaking from our hearts, taking in the energy we were exchanging, taking the time to appreciate the gift of choosing to be present in challenging moments.

—CE

Chapter Nine

SOME THOUGHTS ON

IMPLEMENTATION

Success with the GKI is absolutely not about having fancy PowerPoints or being able to show interesting videos. It's truly not about following step-by-step guidelines; it's all about the facilitator being present, listening to participants and using (being) the NHA while teaching children how to use the NHA on themselves in their own lives.

Celeste led the first year of the Greatness Kids Intervention group without technology and without written activity plans. She sometimes would come up with ways to lead the group while on her way to the meeting place on the middle school campus. As long as she focused on supporting the participants in using the Three Stands of the NHA on themselves and on finding ways for them to share experiences, it worked out pretty well. During that first year, Celeste would often choose to try out new activity ideas for about 10 minutes each during the 29-minute class period. In other sessions, students would spend the half-hour period simply sharing ways they had chosen to reset themselves the night before or during the school day up until that point.

The existence of this book means that the guesswork Celeste worked through won't be necessary for you. Still, it's vital that you feel confident "being the Approach"—that you've spent some time learning and practicing the approach with children and internally with yourself—before you begin to dive into the activities described in these pages.

THE ART AND CRAFT OF LEADING GKI GROUPS —

Reminder once again: BE the Three Stands as you lead the group, whether you're working with students, clients, or your own family members. This can be challenging, especially in the early use of the NHA. It's all about practice, honest reflection, and willingness to continue. It's about trusting the process and looking for what's going well in the moment, even when you don't want to take that look. It's about learning to interweave the Three Stands, sometimes using the distinct Stands within seconds of each other. The stands always optimally exist in concert for your use at all times as needed. Not only will this practice reinforce growth of inner wealth with children in the group, it will make a positive difference in the life of the group leader.

Keep in mind as well that any of these activities can be repeated within the same groups multiple times. Growth will be amplified with repeated sessions.

TIPS FOR FORMING GKI GROUPS
IN AGENCIES, SCHOOLS, AND FAMILIES —

SCHOOLS: For teachers, it would seem easy to include Greatness Kids activities as part of the daily or weekly routine—but the challenge here tends to be finding the time between academic segments. Doing so is entirely worthwhile; students with healthy social-emotional states are much more able to learn.

If you happen to be a school counselor, school psychologist, or school social worker, you could easily work in GKI activities as part of your regularly scheduled time with clients. What can be tricky is setting up a Tier II Intervention with at-risk students from your site, especially if administrators are unfamiliar with NHA. Gift them with an NHA book (even this book), offer up a scheduling plan (including frequency and duration), and explain the purpose of the groups.

For Tier II use of GKI, you would also need a way to identify students needing additional support in the school setting. Many schools run Intervention Team meetings or Teacher Team meetings where students needing additional support are identified using data such as attendance, work completion, grades, and behavior referrals. Often, school counselors, school administrators, and school psychologists are key in helping to identify these students as needing support beyond what all students receive as part of the regular school day (Tier II).

Before beginning each group session, GKI group leaders may want to or need to contact parents in order to briefly explain what the NHA is and how it will be used in the groups. When Celeste ran Tier II GKI groups in the middle school setting, she made individual calls to parents and caregivers to share this information.

School counselors and psychologists can introduce GKI into classrooms struggling with challenging behaviors and intense children. Offer to run a group in that classroom once a week to support students choosing to use their intensity in great ways. Have the teacher participate and take the opportunity to introduce and model use of NHA in a classroom setting for that teacher.

AGENCIES: Many social workers choose to use the Three Stands of NHA during regularly scheduled home visits. Depending on guidelines set forth by agencies, permission may be needed to run groups in homes with families or during counseling sessions. If you need to ask permission from your agency, it would be smart to begin by talking with your supervisor, offering them a gift of the *Transforming the Intense Child Workbook* and explaining that you would like to run groups that will help youth gain higher levels of what we refer to as inner wealth: what kids believe to be true about themselves, self-esteem, levels of confidence and belief in one's self. Also mention suggested guidelines around a specific number of sessions, including as many as you can—ideally once or more per week.

FAMILIES: Of course, when you decide to begin leading GKI activities with your own family, you won't need to ask for permission. You may need to gain buy-in from your partner; if they aren't quite sure about it, invite them to participate or to at least observe. If you implement GKI activities, be sure to use them with ALL family members, not just the most challenging or intense children in the home. Teens may be resistant to any structured family activity and if this is the case for your teen, simply begin by introducing activities in a targeted way during dinner, while riding in the car, or in any other situation that may appear less structured.

FREQUENCY AND DURATION OF SESSIONS —

We've seen GKI groups held as often as four to five days per week and up to 60 minutes per session, or as seldom as once per week for 30 minutes per meeting. While greater frequency and longer duration tend to yield the best results, most of the activities listed in this book can be completed in a 30-minute time period. A few of the activities involving projects may need extended time or completion over two sessions. If time runs short, continue the activity where it was left off during the last session.

ATTENTION, AUTHENTICITY AND INTENTION —

A few pointers to support your success as a GKI leader:

Pay deep attention. While leading families, small groups, or even large groups through GKI activities, facilitators should practice being fully *present*: intentionally showing up with total presence and attention, resetting along the way as needed. If you, as facilitator, notice that you are resetting more often than you think you should be, that's okay—what's probably true is that you are 100% on the right track.

The goal is to drop into presence deeply enough that you feel connected to participants, and that they, in return, will feel seen, heard, and important to you. Sometimes, especially with children experiencing trauma in their lives, walls of invisible protection have been built, and this level of presence is required to give them an adequate sense of safety to broach those protective walls. When youth appear unable to accept being connected, notch up the stands and don't give up!

I have come to sense that at the root of all energy is love; and that, on the way to better and purer versions of that in my own life, every next level of my ability to be "present" is the energy of love that is manifesting in relation to all I do and say in this world. My wish is that the Nurtured Heart Approach accelerates that unfolding level of presence for all involved.

As adults learning and using the NHA, we give that loving energy of presence in the form of our choices of words and actions. By bringing this approach directly to children via the GKI, we empower them to manifest presence and love in a world that is desperate for such answers to life's persistent issues. We help children to see themselves as being lovingly and appreciatively present at ever greater levels: through interactions that are purposefully clear about life's challenges with the realm of NO (what we don't want to give our presence to) and the realm of YES (what we do want to appreciatively love and honor). And through these two streams of influence, they gain so much clarity about how they want to navigate their lives.

—HG

Radiate authenticity. Authenticity gives off an energy that kids of all ages are able to read and feel, especially younger children. An authentic adult is one who can be trusted, and building trust (between youth and adults and also between peers) in GKI groups is vital. Resetting is a wonderful way to show up with authenticity; never be afraid to reset yourself in front of the group, to show emotion, and to be honest with your comments while facilitating.

In moments of being authentic that may be uncomfortable for others to watch, know that kids may laugh, roll their eyes, show closed-off body language, and even make fun of the authenticity you are demonstrating. This is your cue to reset yourself and keep on going! Allow yourself to feel the struggle, reset, and use the energy in the next moment for getting back on task: giving the next positive recognition or focusing once again on being present and aware. Leading groups is not about control; it is about proving that you (the leader) and the participants are in this together.

Remember the intention of building Inner Wealth. Find strategies to remind yourself often of the ultimate intention of the Greatness Kids Initiative: increasing children's inner wealth. As you work to keep this intention alive, know that the inevitable moments of struggle—children's off-task behaviors or inappropriate language, your own self-doubt, or other challenges—are opportunities for you to access the Three Stands. As you ride the waves of negative behaviors and use the Stands effectively, you will find yourself more easily slipping into this as default mode in your life outside of GKI groups. When faced with a wave of negativity, know that a miracle of transformation is almost definitely right around the corner as long as you keep leaning hard into the Three Stands.

A simple mantra to use as a reminder of all three of these points is: *I am the greatness of being present with authenticity and intention.*

FINE-TUNING RECOGNITION TECHNIQUES FOR MAXIMUM IMPACT

Where a child is struggling to participate in positive relationship with adults, or is used to receiving adult attention only for negative behaviors, the use of a long, detailed recognition may challenge the child to take it all in. They may be more likely to resist and defend. Under these circumstances, a quick Active Recognition may be just as powerful as a longer Experiential or Proactive Recognition. Get back to notching up your use of the longer appreciations as soon as you can.

Overall, take notice of the ways in which children in your groups receive recognitions most readily, especially when they are new to NHA and GKI. Some young people prefer being recognized out loud in front of their peers and siblings; others appreciate a more quiet and private delivery; some even appreciate having a recognition written on a Post-It note and placed on the desk or table near them. As children begin to understand that they really do possess positive qualities, most come to be able to hear recognitions in front of groups or families, but this may take time and care. Allow for this. And most of all: remember to keep making the most of every opportunity to energize children in your care, and to not let a child's resistance throw you off-purpose in your Stands.

GKI IS FOR KIDS OF ALL AGES (INCLUDING ADULTS)

The experience of leading and having others lead Greatness Kids Initiative groups since 2010 has demonstrated for sure that sharing NHA with children and teens of all ages is beneficial. All children benefit from learning to use the Three Stands on themselves.

These activities are not only for children and teens who are actively struggling with their own inner wealth. Discovering next levels of inner wealth is a lifelong process, and anyone can benefit from this exploration— any age, in any setting. Youth who are not actively struggling can benefit too. Students have demonstrated growth in all grade levels (including pre-school) in general education, special education, intervention, alternative education, counseling, family, and therapy settings.

GKI activities are absolutely useful in work with adults as well. The intention is the same as in use with children: to provide a deeper understanding of the Approach through experiential activities. Adults enjoy the activities as much as children do in groups.

A few years back, I presented NHA to a group of senior citizens living in a retirement community. I planned the training without being sure what to expect, knowing that although many of the seniors probably had children in their lives, the training would focus on using the Three Stands in their own lives and with each other.

Most of the seniors in the group showed up ready to be engaged, were interested, and were absolutely willing to share their own experiences. They appeared to thoroughly enjoy sharing their own qualities of greatness and providing evidence of those qualities. Even quiet and reserved (and maybe skeptical) participants chose to participate fully by the end of the training.

It was magical. Special stories of important lifetime memories were shared and appreciated in a new way. Where self-doubt and regrets arose about occurrences from the past, we were able to dive into what was great about those experiences. Struggles and successes related to participants' career histories were shared, and I was able to recognize them for positive differences that they made in the world. No question: Greatness Kids Initiative groups are for more than just kids.

—CE

Chapter Ten

GREATNESS BREATHING

For years, Howard Glasser has been cultivating a greatness practice for himself. It has woven together a unique form of breathwork (Greatness Breathing) and the internal use of the Nurtured Heart Approach stands and energizing techniques.

As he worked internally with this vitality-building combination of breath, energy, and inner talk, he began to bring it to a handful of close associates through a mentoring process designed to guide Advanced Trainers to next levels of 'being the Approach.' In this chapter, Howard walks us through an introduction to this greatness practice.

As adults came to me seeking to learn the *'outer'* Nurtured Heart Approach, I usually found that they were in search of effective ways to help intense kids channel their energy into fuel for their greatness. My big 'aha!' came when I realized how the newly hatched *'inner'* Nurtured Heart Approach could serve this cause.

In their jobs of running programs for the behaviorally most challenging youth, I've seen adults at high risk of burnout. How could I support them in sustaining their own energy in this work? I knew that a big part of this equation would be a deep practice of maintaining and notching up the Stands in their interactions with the youth in their care – and that they would be best equipped to do this if they had an effective personal practice of doing so within themselves: a way of interacting with and nourishing themselves deeply and consistently.

I developed a mentorship model that would enable me to share a process I'd been working with privately for years – where I practice using the breath, visualization, and exquisitely energizing 'inner greatness' talk to take advantage of all the energies coursing through me on a given day (energies that my previous studies in clinical therapies would have me either perseverating upon or ineffectually trying to shed). I had cultivated ways to use these energies to grow my own greatness: to move this energy exactly to where I know it will do the most good.

My rationale: if we can personally, internally cultivate exactly the thing we are wanting for our children, we can better recognize and work with the ongoing challenges faced by any person of any age when waves of energy meet waves of resistance. We become better able to assist, encourage, and support the children with whom we are working, in a way that dignifies and uplifts both the children and ourselves. We can also be less prone to throw in the towel and more able to dig deeper and notch up when the going gets tough. In 2016, I began to bring this internal Nurtured Heart Approach (aka 'greatness practice') into my training programs.

Ultimately, I recognized that my end goal with refining and mentoring trainers in this work was to prepare those who have the great honor of working directly with the most intense children to bring these practices directly to those children. I also now see it as an advanced-level teaching in a Greatness Kids Initiative; a kind of 'resetting-plus' practice.

After all: if my premise of intensity being a gift is indeed true, these most intense children could tap into the gift of all gifts if given the right practices and tools. The potential here is especially vast for highly intense young people. It reminds me of the potential of geothermal energy—the heat beneath the earth's surface that some countries intelligently access and use to cleanly power whole cities.

We can teach the most intense children to tap directly into this source within themselves. The very energies that could otherwise be overwhelming can now be useful and purposeful. We can set these children free as self-sufficient in perpetuating their own greatness.

How? By using the NHA with them, of course; but also by directly teaching them to use the breath and to use the NHA on *themselves* to mindfully convert all energies— good, great, bad, and ugly–toward the cultivation and nurturance of their own greatness.

Ultimately, the practices described here are next-level self-resets: effective, clean, efficient ways to reset and renew to the gifts of the next moment.

A GENERAL INTRODUCTION TO GREATNESS BREATHING –

Greatness Breathing's wisdom is drawn from that of many traditions – many of which I've studied as an eternal student of awakening my own consciousness into greatness. It focuses on and celebrates the power of the heart to handle everything the universe throws at us (consider that your greatness has handled everything you've had to overcome until now). Our hearts handle beautifully the daily flow and range of energies that enter our lives: our joy and happiness as well as our frustration, despair, sorrow, and worry.

It is a practice built around my recognition that I could choose to not struggle against feelings I would rather not have or that feel like *too much*; to not overthink or analyze them, to refuse (Stand One!) to go into CSI (Crime Scene Investigation) mode in an effort to rationally dissipate an emotional state that is causing me discomfort. Of course, these overwhelming energies still show up uninvited; however, as soon as I get clear that they have arrived in a form I am not willing to let linger, I let this inform my inner limits (Stand Three). Instead, I choose to drink the energy of those strong feelings into my heart, where I can use my heart's power to reset and renew. This leads me to an experience of converting rough or challenging energies into the great aspects of me that can better serve myself and others in the moment.

My hope is that you can work with this within yourself for some time– until you have felt its benefit–and that you can then teach it directly to children in your care.

INTRODUCTORY GREATNESS BREATHING –

I think of the breath as having three segments: the in-breath, the top of the breath, and the out-breath. Each segment has a role in Greatness Breathing.

IN-BREATH/INSPIRE: The first part of the breath is the drinking-in of energy, a time to welcome in all the energies that have found their way to our lives and to feel them as fresh fuel–the moment where we *inspire* (a word from the Latin *in* + *spirare,* meaning "To breathe into"). The connotations here are clear: we have the option to use the gift of every in-breath, and all our energies, as sources of inspiration.

To start your own Greatness Breathing journey, begin to practice inspiration through the in-breath. Drink in each in-breath as energy.

TOP OF THE BREATH/CONSPIRE: This is the choice point: where you consciously decide–set an intention–to use the power of your inspiration to super-energize the parts of you that you want to grow; to reset to greatness; to focus mindfully on cultivating more of what already exists, and of what we want to begin to cultivate within and for ourselves.

OUT-BREATH/EXPIRE: The out-breath is where we can consciously energize next levels of greatness, moving/breathing this renewed energy of what we are now conspiring to out to all the trillion cells that make up who and what we are. In breathing out this previously challenging energy with this clarified and renewed message of greatness, we *expire* to who we were and who we are now becoming by sending this greatness energy out to our world—within and even beyond the confines of our energy field.

Here's how this whole thing works in real life.

Let's say I am worried about some project I am working on, or mad about something someone said.

On my next inbreath, I find a way to take in those waves of energy and embrace them – use them as *inspiration* – rather than brace against them. The most useful envisioning I've found is to imagine a trillion sub-microscopic straws extending from my heart center to every single cell in my body and daring to drink in this tough energy with a fierce determination to convert it in my heart. I feel like I am extracting the very energy that could become stagnant in my cells and readying to use it as fuel for my next levels of greatness.

At the top of the breath, I *conspire:* I feel deeply into that very energy and search for the greatness that will be medicinal to me in the moments to follow. Sometimes, it's right there like a neon sign; sometimes, it takes a few more inspiring breaths or a series of breaths. Sometimes it feels like I'm just taking a wild guess at what greatness will provide the magic in this situation or emotion that was bothering me. I prepare to send this potent energy back to each one those trillion cells—to nourish all them all in greatness.

On the outbreath, essentially *expiring* to 'life as I knew it,' I imagine sending that now nourishing energy from my heart to every cell of my body. I imagine sending it with powerful messages like, "I am the greatness of understanding," "I am the greatness of patience," "I am the greatness of unflappable empowerment," or whatever else might apply to help move the needle of my growing greatness.

That's all there is to it. It's a process of consciously using the breath and the power of the mind and heart to transform what might have been spun into a maelstrom of negativity into nourishment. It's a way of metabolizing energies that could potentially metastasize.

This practice of growing greatness through the breath at any moment it is needed has helped my life enormously. Every time I choose to engage in this practice, I step into owning my greatness. Problems and issues from previous days, weeks and months seem to dissolve or become much easier to solve.

We can gift young people with this as an empowering life process that will help them with all life sends their way–a process meant to guide young people to handle strong feelings proactively; to teach them to move, through consistent practice, from a "fight-flight-freeze" default with strong emotional states to a revised default of using that energy to grow their own greatness.

All children can benefit from Greatness Breathing practice. They (more readily than adults) can learn to be the growers of their own greatness in ways that will light up their runways for living productive and fruitful lives. These children can learn a life skill that won't keep them from having life issues…but that will prepare them to use their energy to go forward better and stronger every time.

One of my silly ways of checking in with the people I teach this process to is to jokingly inquire, "Has *Greatness Breathing* ruined your life yet?" If ever anyone answers "yes," I'll go on notice; for now, I believe wholeheartedly that it is worth learning and teaching to children in our care.

A Nurtured Heart Approach trainer shared a story about using Greatness Breathing with an especially challenging student. This 15-year-old boy was extremely intimidating in his physique and had done serious and frightening damage to staff (intimidation, physical harm and sexual assault). When this trainer courageously worked to guide this young man through Greatness Breathing, he did not close his eyes, but was able to sit with the feelings of anger that he had previously acted out. Through practicing this unique form of breathing with the help and mentoring of this trainer, he was able to stop punching the walls; he stopped threatening to kill staff; and he was able to identify the real emotions he was feeling—which were primarily sadness and loss. He was then able to share the greatness of emerging coping skills that he planned to use when he felt these kinds of intense emotions (talking to staff, writing music).

If I were working as a supervisor to this trainer or as a colleague, I would actively want to do a few sentences of robust appreciation. I would want to say what I witnessed or knew of this incredibly transformative situation and I would want to give her credit: "I noticed an enormous change with the young man. He is so much more kind and wise in his behaviors and his actions and I deeply appreciated the work you have been doing with him. I appreciate your great courage and resolve to help even the most difficult and challenging kids who come into our program, and this reveals to me your amazing strength of conviction and resolve as well as the depth of your caring and the love you have for these children. You are the greatness of being an inspired and powerful transformer of even the toughest kids and you have shown us all here what is possible."

— HG

Chapter Eleven

THE TRUTH ABOUT

OUR CHILDREN AND NHA

The very first Greatness Kids group was made up of 120 academically successful middle school students with high grades and state testing scores. The purpose of the group was to teach these students how to use NHA strategies to support their peers in academic intervention classes.

As mentioned earlier in this book, the second type of Greatness Kids group was created to help students needing additional behavior and social-emotional support. The intention of this group was to teach these students how to use NHA strategies on themselves in order to build their own inner wealth.

For one year, these groups overlapped. Celeste chose to lead both groups through the same NHA activities, each in their own sessions. There was an activity where students were asked to read cards demonstrating how adults spoke to them in negative and positive ways throughout a day. It was eye-opening to see how similar the situations of the more prototypically 'successful' kids and those of the students needing support were. It was clear that ALL students, whether successful or struggling, shared the same ideas and concerns; that all of them needed to be seen, reflected, and encouraged to see themselves in greatness.

One student in the high-achieving group shared that when she earned straight A's on her report card, her parents appeared to be proud—yet, they never said much about what it took for her to earn such fantastic grades.

If she came home with an A- or B+ on a test, her parents responded with lectures about trying harder and studying more, and with statements like "You're better than an A minus or B plus." She was threatened with the possibility of losing privileges and was told to pay more attention in class. She shared that talk like this was the opposite of motivational. Although she recognized that her parents were speaking to her in this way because they cared, the end result was her feeling bad about herself.

Other students in the mentoring group shared stories about comments made by teachers that impacted them for days, even weeks. Even small positive comments could go a long way: in one case, a teacher made a very brief positive comment about a good grade on a test, and the student said that it made her day. Most of the time, this student shared, teachers would say nothing to her about high test scores. Another student shared that one tiny negative comment like "Better try harder next time" or "Did you study for this test?" would have an extreme negative effect that lingered for weeks.

Across levels of achievement, students participating in the initial Greatness Kids Intervention group shared stories that were very similar: they were beginning to notice that even the smallest negative comments made by adults in their lives had tremendous impact. They also were intensely aware that in general, comments about anything they did well were few and far between. They shared that their efforts to do and be better were overshadowed by lectures including statements like, "Where did we go wrong with you?" and "How did we get to this point?" and "I wish you would just try to be a better kid." Across the whole program, students shared similar stories of needing to rely on their peers for any kind of positive recognition–although often, these comments were of a superficial nature, about clothing or personal style.

It became clear that all kids need to have their inner wealth supported and that all, no matter how successful or unsuccessful, can learn to accept positive recognitions. Every student served in that first GKI struggled with accepting and believing great things about themselves—with owning their greatness.

If we aren't willing to take a stand to support ALL children in a way that inspires positive growth, the alternative is that a cycle of negativity sometimes leading to sadness, anger, isolation and violence. With levels of anxiety and hopelessness at an all-time high for children across all demographics, and with so many pressing personal, local, and global issues facing the next generation, it's easy for adults to feel helpless and hopeless themselves. Bringing the NHA to as many people as possible is one of the best ways we've found to feel as though we are making a meaningful difference.

How does this difference play out? Transformation seen in children participating in GKI groups across ages and settings include: higher levels of participation and engagement in school and within the family, increased levels of confidence, improved grades, increased self-awareness, willingness to form friendships and relationships, the courage to cultivate their passion, gaining the bravery needed to take academic risks, increased levels of honesty, deep appreciation, gratitude, improved behavior, higher levels of concentration, increased ability to solve social challenges and an increased sense of happiness.

I recommend, with all my heart, that you deeply and robustly appreciate yourself as you do this work. You deserve it for your great intention to help the children in your care, and you deserve it for your willingness to go the extra mile to even consider all that is here in the Greatness Kids Initiative. I know I appreciate your desire to help children to find themselves and to grow in their skills and abilities. I appreciate the love in your heart to take on this noble work, and in turn I truly hope you appreciate yourself for this.

To me, this and so much more reveals your inspiration to make this world a better place, one child at a time. I truly hope you can see this amazing inspiration in yourself. You are great love, great inspiration, great empowerment, great wisdom, and great willingness to be the change…and I truly hope you can see and own this greatness in yourself and so much more.

— HG

ABOUT THE AUTHORS

CELESTE ELSEY

Celeste Elsey, MA Special Education, has been an Advanced Trainer in the Nurtured Heart Approach® (NHA) for the past 10 years. She has trained parents, caregivers, therapists, social workers and educators across the United States. Celeste leads Greatness Kids Initiative groups, teaching youth how to use NHA in their own lives. Celeste is motivated to promote NHA through her love of public speaking and supporting others to make a positive difference in the lives of children. Celeste's background in education includes teaching special education in middle school, alternative education in middle school and high school as well being an instructional coach for teachers at all grade levels. She is currently a special education teacher in a K-8 setting. She and her husband Joe reside in California, have raised three boys, have one grandson and use NHA in all aspects of their lives.

MELISSA LOWENSTEIN

Melissa Lynn Lowenstein, M.Ed., is an educator, writer, editor, and creative artist who has authored over 25 books, including many of those in the Nurtured Heart Approach library. She also works as Programs Coordinator and Core Facilitator with Santa Barbara, California non-profit AHA!, working as part of a team to create and implement an award-winning social-emotional learning (SEL), creativity, and social conscience curriculum to thousands of youth and hundreds of educators and youth providers each year. She lives with her teen children and partner in Santa Barbara.

HOWARD GLASSER

Howard Glasser is Founder of the Children's Success Foundation and creator of the Nurtured Heart Approach®. Howard studied family therapy, clinical studies and educational leadership and has emerged as a voice for children's greatness. His body of work has been inspired from his work with some of the most intense and challenging children. He has been referred to as one of the more influential living persons working to reduce children's reliance on psychiatric medications. He has been featured on CNN and in *Esquire Magazine,* and is a sought-after keynote speaker at conferences in areas of treatment and education. He is the author of 15 books, including *Transforming the Difficult Child, Notching Up the Nurtured Heart Approach,* and *Igniting Greatness.* His Nurtured Heart Approach has been successfully adopted by the state of New Jersey's Coordinated System of Care, is being examined as a model of care by other states, and is being researched by both Rutgers University and the University of Arizona's Zuckerman School of Public Health, with findings soon to be published. He currently teaches certification trainings on his method and teaches at Andrew Weil's renowned program at the University of Arizona's School of Integrative Medicine, and in the department of Transformational Wellness at U of A's School of Public Health.